The Bag Boutique

CW00348203

Dedication

I love sewing and I have been doing it for a very long time. My Nana taught me to sew on her original Singer treadle sewing machine when I was eight years old and my Mum taught me the finer points of hand sewing. I inherited my Nana's machine and I still have it today. It is full of memories for me.

This book is for you.

20 bright and beautiful bags to sew

The Bag Boutique

DEBBIE VON GRABLER-CROZIER

SEARCH PRESS

Acknowledgements

This is the part of the book that I dreaded writing because the thought of missing someone out would be too terrible to contemplate. So let us begin and see how we go. Firstly, thank you to Rob, Tristan and Mum for your support and putting up with quite a lot, to be fair. Thank you for cooking meals when we would have all starved to death and being very flexible about when we got to enjoy them. There is no way that this book would be here at all without you three.

Some people have been awfully generous about supplying me with beautiful things so that these bags would look great. To the wonderful team at Hantex and Pat and Walter Bravo of Art Gallery Fabrics, a huge thank you! There are a great many bags in this book owing their look to AGF and I cannot find the words to describe how I feel when I look at them. My heart is singing.

Thank you also to Jayne from Makower UK for the splendiferous Christmas fabric for the Helge messenger bag. Sometimes a bag and a fabric are just crying out for one another.

The foundations for my bags all come from Vlieseline and they are a keystone, the necessary undergarments to lift the bag to its coveted handmade status. I now know that my bags cannot live without them, so Sharron, thank you so much for endlessly traipsing out to the warehouse armed with scissors for me! There must have been times when you thought that I was eating the stuff!

These bags are not all hand sewn of course and I have the most beautiful sewing machine in the world to help to bring it all together. To the lovely peeps at Janome UK, thank you so (sew?) much for my Janome Memory Craft 8200 QCP! I have always loved Janome and I am more besotted than ever.

And of course, to Katie French, Becky Robbins, May Corfield, Juan Hayward, Marrianne Miall, Stacy Grant and Paul Bricknell – thank you all for playing your part and making me look like a real writer! I look forward to more of this on our creative journey together.

Finally, I must thank my magazine editors, all twenty of you across the world, for being patient with some of the 'day job' deadlines as the important dates drew near.

A good and professional book is never the work of just one person – I even have to thank my two Cocker Spaniels, Sally and Daisy, who have sat beside me in silent support and bullied me relentlessly when I strayed from my desk. I owe you both homemade dog biscuits. Heart-shaped ones. With fried chicken liver bits.

I think that I might love you all!

First published in 2018

Search Press Limited
Wellwood, North Farm Road,
Tunbridge Wells, Kent TN2 3DR

Text copyright ©
Debbie von Grabler-Crozier 2018

Photographs by Stacy Grant: cover, 1, 2–3, 5, 6, 7, 8, 10, 21t, 28t, 29b, 30br, 36, 37, 38, 43tr, 44, 46, 47, 48, 52, 55, 56, 61, 62, 66, 69, 70, 73b, 74, 77, 78, 81, 83, 84, 88, 91, 92, 94, 99, 100, 104, 105b, 106, 108b, 111, 112, 115, 116, 119, 120, 123, 124, 127b, 128, 131, 132, 135t, 136, 141, 142–143b, 144

Photographs by Paul Bricknell: 9, 11, 13, 14, 15, 17, 18, 19, 20, 21 (steps), 22, 23, 24, 25, 26, 27, 28 (steps), 29 (steps), 30 (steps), 31, 32, 33, 34, 35, 39, 40, 41, 42, 43 (steps), 45, 50, 51, 54, 58, 59, 60, 64, 65, 67, 68, 71, 72, 73t, 76, 80, 82, 86, 87, 89, 90, 93, 96, 97, 102, 103, 105t, 108t, 109, 110, 114, 118, 121, 122, 126, 127t, 130, 133, 134, 135b, 138, 139, 140, 142t

Photographs and design copyright ©
Search Press Ltd 2018

All rights reserved. No part of this book, text, photographs or illustrations may be reproduced or transmitted in any form or by any means by print, photoprint, microfilm, microfiche, photocopier, internet or in any way known or as yet unknown, or stored in a retrieval system, without written permission obtained beforehand from Search Press.

ISBN: 978-1-78221-430-4

The Publishers and author can accept no responsibility for any consequences arising from the information, advice or instructions given in this publication.

Readers are permitted to reproduce any of the items/patterns in this book for their personal use, or for the purposes of selling for charity, free of charge and without the prior permission of the Publishers. Any use of the items/patterns for commercial purposes is not permitted without the prior permission of the Publishers.

Suppliers
For details of suppliers, please visit the Search Press website: www.searchpress.com.

Printed in China through Asia Pacific Offset

Publishers' note
All the step-by-step photographs in this book feature the author, Debbie von Grabler-Crozier.

Contents

Ina

Introduction	**6**
Materials	**8**
Fabrics	8
Felts	9
Threads	10
Trims and shop-bought embellishments	11
Haberdashery and hardware	12
Equipment	16
Techniques	**18**
Seaming	18
Finishing seams and lining	19
Binding edges	20
Patchworking	21
Inserting a zip	22
Making box corners	25
Clipping, notching and cutting across corners	26
Making bias binding	27
Applying bias binding	28
Piping	29
Inserting patch pockets	31
Straps, handles and tabs	32
Embellishment	**35**
Embroidery	35
Appliqué	39
Crocheted flowers	41
Adapting charms to make brooches	42
Beaded charms	43
Making labels	44

The Bags	**46**
Lorle	48
Liesl	52
Shirley	56
Tilde	62
Hannah	66
Claudia	70
Lotte	74
Minna	78
Anna Lena	84
Margaret	88
Christa	94
Ingrid	100
Ina	106
Gertrude	112
Trixie	116
Sylvia	120
Dörte	124
Kirsten	128
Helge	132
Karin	136
Index	**144**
Templates	

Shirley

Ingrid

Sylvia

INTRODUCTION

Clothes may maketh the man but a great bag will definitely complete a woman's outfit! I love that a new bag can be practical, fun and interesting all at the same time – and it can spruce up your wardrobe. As a rule, you won't need very much in the way of fabric when making your own bags. Unless you are going for a suitcase or a massively oversized model's bag, you can produce something fabulous with fat quarters, eighths and even scraps – what's not to love there? But a bag has to be more than that, so we add embellishments. I love personalised labels, keyrings and flowers, which say 'this bag is all mine and I love it!'; one of the bags in this book even wishes you a happy day when you open the flap (Sylvia, see page 120). Learning to sew your own bags means that you can make individual masterpieces; change fabrics for a new look or swap an embellishment and you have a wonderfully personal result to either carry proudly or give as a gift. Above all, although some of the bags may look a little bit complicated, when you filter down the steps, each one is quite achievable, and anyone from a confident beginner up should be able to produce something special.

It is usual at this point to wish you well on your sewing journey and to tell you that 'I hope that you enjoy making these bags as much as I have enjoyed designing them'... but I really do mean just that! A bag is supposed to bring joy, both to the carrier and to the onlooker. Feel happiness every time you get to leave your house carrying something that is yours alone.

So, let's get on with it then – let's make bags! With love,

Debbie x

MATERIALS

Although you will require a number of bits and pieces to construct a usable bag, none of these things is so obscure that you cannot find it either in the shops or on a good website. You possibly have quite a lot of these items already. Sometimes, searching in the hardware store will give you good results too. Things like 'O'-rings and plastic tubing used for handles can be found at a fraction of the cost, so go on a hardware treasure hunt!

FABRICS

The basis of any bag is the fabric that you use. Fabric will bring your bag alive, and each fabric will give a bag a different personality. Bag making takes time and at the end of it you will have produced something that should be a friend for a very long time, so use the best quality fabric that you can afford. Most of the bags in this book use cotton quilting fabrics and you can get them in any sewing or quilting supply store. Bookmark your favourite sites online and subscribe to newsletters. Then, when they are having a sale or you receive a voucher, go to town with your plans for fabric.

The best way to choose your fabrics is to 'audition' them by laying them out together and seeing if they play nicely. It's always satisfying to use fabrics from your stash, although of course sometimes you might just want a particular colour or print. If the fabrics are really conflicting, try putting a plain in between. More often than not, a beautiful accent fabric already in your stash can be used by carefully buying another 'blender' to go with it. There is no such thing as the wrong fabric – usually just the wrong application. Make sure your stash includes some plains or 'solids' as they are known. These are great for piping and binding and generally accentuating your work.

Tip

To choose which plain fabric to use with a print, look at the colours of the print. The plain should be whichever colour is used least in the print fabric. This stops it from becoming overwhelming.

Sometimes bags work better made from slightly thicker fabrics, or from furnishing-weight fabrics and linens. Search in shops for remnants that may not be big enough to make a full set of curtains but may be large enough for a bag – never miss an opportunity to rummage.

No modern sewing book would be complete without at least mentioning the recycling option when it comes to fabric gathering. Look at your own unwanted clothes and those of your family – with appropriate permission of course! Charity or thrift shops provide another source of fabric. The main rule of thumb is to avoid synthetics and any fabrics that smell particularly funny.

FELTS

I use felt in a few ways but mainly for embellishment and flowers. Unless you put them side by side, it can be quite difficult to tell the difference between acrylic and wool felt. The test of quality isn't really about what it looks like on the day of making – it is about wear. Wool wears better than acrylic. You seldom get the pills and furring with wool that you get with acrylic. When they are used together, the difference can be quite striking, so my advice is:

• use either wool *or* acrylic in any one project
• use the best of either that you can afford.

Tip

Because the amounts needed are usually small, look for scrap bags online. You cannot choose the colours, but if you aren't looking for a particular one, this can really save you money.

One thing that is very obvious when wool and acrylic felts are used together is the colour. Wool is capable of giving much more muted tones. They look classy. Enough said. But – and there is always a but – if you want bright you always have the option of acrylic.

Tip

When buying grey felt opt for a marl instead of flat grey. For some reason it has more depth to it and, in my opinion, just looks better.

Mostly your felt needs will be answered by squares and scraps, but every now and then felt forms a main part of a bag, such as Lotte on pages 74–77. In this setting, wool felt is the only choice. Not only will it wear better (no fluffing and pilling), but you also need it in a larger piece. Felt like this is bought by the metre and it comes in several thicknesses and lots of wonderful colours. Around 2mm ($1/16$in) thick is a good rule of thumb – remember that you will use several layers in a bag and your poor, long-suffering sewing machine has to go through all of them.

THREADS

Just about every sewing book and magazine you pick up now will tell you about hugely expensive, name-brand threads and warn you on pain of death that if you don't use them, something bad will happen. At this point I just want to say that some of the bags in this book have been made with expensive named threads and others haven't. I have used the cheapest possible on some because that was the thread that I had or the colour that was needed. Obviously, use the best thread that you can afford, but if you want to try out your skills, consider using own-brand threads.

By and large, I use white or ecru thread for most applications. The exceptions are topstitching, some quilting and putting on woven ribbon. It looks more professional then to change to a coordinating thread. This is of course unless you want the topstitching as a feature.

No thread section would be complete without mentioning stranded embroidery cottons and perle coton. These are the colouring-in pencils of the sewing world. They will help you write messages and create a world of loveliness in flowers,

but what is the difference between the two? Stranded cotton or embroidery floss are the same thing; they are basically cotton (usually) on a skein which comes in a bundle of six separable threads. Rarely will a pattern require you to use all six threads – this would be too chunky. The pattern will tell you how many threads to use and you simply cut off a length of about 45cm (17$^3/_4$in) (any longer and they can tangle) and then separate out the amount needed. Thread the needle and you are ready to roll.

Perle coton – not a spelling error, actually the proper title is *perlé coton à broder* – is a thicker embroidery thread. It comes in three thicknesses, 5 (the thickest), 8 (medium) and 12 (finer). Even #12 is not as fine as stranded embroidery floss though. Here again, specific patterns will tell you which one to use for each effect.

You can buy either of these products wherever you buy your sewing supplies and I'll hazard a guess that if you are not an embroidery person, you have walked past the stand a thousand times!

TRIMS AND SHOP-BOUGHT EMBELLISHMENTS

These are the bits second only to fabric that gladden the heart of the maker! Trims include buttons, ribbons, lace and all sorts of pretty things. Here, as always, the message is to get the best quality that you can possibly manage. These sorts of trim draw the eye and if they are not nice it can sink your project.

I love searching online for buttons especially (I have a bit of a thing for buttons). I remember as a child playing with my great-aunt's button box and, when she died, it was put into a pile of things to be sold or given away. I couldn't believe it! I ran straight to my mother and begged to be allowed to keep it. I still have the box and the buttons today and some are nearly 100 years old! When you think about vintage, a button is allowed to be a bit rough around the edges, but there is a very big difference between cheap and nasty and old and worn. Somehow you can just tell.

Lace is another beautiful thing which, in the right setting, can look simply marvellous. My favourite is cotton lace – you know the heavier sort that looks crocheted? It is so much more pleasing to the eye than the light nylon stuff. But be careful – unfortunately, the wrong trims and sometimes the wrong colours can make your project look dated (think dusty pink ruffles on everything in the 1980s).

Jumbo ric-rac is another must-have and it teams so well with ribbon. I prefer to tuck it under a piece of coordinating woven ribbon. On its own it can look a bit less sophisticated to my eyes.

Ribbons complete the picture and they can be the slightly pricier woven ones or own-brand ones from a chain store. What matters is how you use them. Make bows or use them to separate one section of fabric from another – they make an instant impact.

Tip

If you travel anywhere at all, look out for local trims and fancies. They are not expensive as souvenirs and they are practically weightless in a suitcase, taking up very little room. I have found beautiful woven ribbons and metal buttons in Germany and Austria that we cannot get in the UK. They become a beautiful memento of a trip away.

HABERDASHERY AND HARDWARE

ZIPS

The bags in this book use good-quality plastic zips because I am after their colours and the fact that they can be easily shortened if necessary. When buying a zip, always go for one slightly longer than you need – it is really easy to make them shorter.

If your zip refuses to run smoothly, rub a small amount of pure beeswax (available in a block) over the teeth and then press it with a slightly warm iron under a cloth; always use the cloth and never have the iron too hot. The iron will melt the beeswax, which will trickle into the teeth of the zip and lubricate it. I have saved a project or two this way. I always tell myself to test every zip in the shop but…

INTERFACING

To be fair, we could have a book on this alone! But let's keep it simple for now and say that if you have four or five types, you can make all of the bags in the book. That seems a lot, but consider that if you cut open a shop-bought bag, you would be blown away by how many hidden layers are in there. The same with a suit jacket. That and that alone can be what lifts an article from the dreaded 'homemade' to the very coveted 'handmade'.

First though, what is interfacing and why is it needed? Interfacing is the investment part of your bag and without it, the bag would have no structure. Never consider making a bag or purse without at least some wadding/batting behind the fabric because fabrics alone have no strength – no, not even the furnishing-weight ones. Interfacing works magic on fabric, allowing it to stand up unaided or sit comfortably. Interfacing is like a good bra, in fact – a saggy old one can ruin the line of the most beautiful outfit. It doesn't matter how beautiful or top drawer your fabric, if you do not have the proper foundation, it will be droopy and sad. Interfacing works very hard behind the scenes to make your fabrics look luxe.

Interfacing falls into one of two groups as a rule: sew-in and fusible. Sew-in is the same both sides and you have to sew it to the fabric to achieve the desired result. This is always done with a half or even quarter normal seam allowance. Sometimes, a sew-in interfacing that is soft and dense (like Thermolam) is needed for a quilted part of a bag.

Fusible interfacing has a glue on one side and you iron it to the wrong side of the fabric. The glue side will always be either rough or shiny and you can tell it from the 'normal' side. Always iron it on under a damp pressing cloth (the glue will play havoc with the plate of your iron, as will synthetic interfacing, which melts if it comes into contact with direct heat). I find this better than steam and you have much more control. Invest in a spray bottle for ironing. You will use it again and again.

My favourite interfacings are a foam one (Style-Vil) which is a sew-in type; Decovil I Light and H630, which are fusible types of wadding/batting; Thermolam, which is an acrylic sew-in type, perfect for quilting onto; and Decovil (regular), which is great for bases. I also use Bundfix tape over and over for handles and S320 for all of my pockets. G740 is a light woven fusible type, which is great for adding just that little extra and works a treat for stabilising linen to stop it fraying. These are all Vlieseline products and I use them constantly, but other brands and products are available – so do your research, try out different samples and see what works for you.

I also use a plastic canvas mesh for bases (it depends on the sort of base – the pattern will always give the specifics). Vlieseline's S133 is a super-heavy-duty sew-in interfacing also great for bases but it can be a struggle on a curve. Cut it smaller than the base piece itself and keep it out of the seam allowance. It is actually meant for baseball cap peaks so it is super-strong stuff. I am sure that you have heard this before but never use cardboard. It doesn't matter how heavy it feels, it will not stand up to wear, it isn't washable and it isn't rain-proof. If you cannot get plastic mesh, foam board is the next best thing. The one that you are after has a foam core and two very shiny sides. You can cut this to size with a craft knife.

Finally, while we are talking interfacing, you will see that some of the patterns have multiple layers of different sorts. This is not a misprint. It is very necessary because each piece of interfacing performs a separate function. Sometimes, you need strength and squishiness so you might use two layers of H630, for example, with Decovil in between. Or you might start with H630 fused to the back of a bag, quilt that and then add a layer of Style-Vil foam to make the bag hold its shape. Where more than one type of interfacing is used in a project, I have been very careful to specify what type I'm referring to at each point – to make life easy for all of us!

> ## Tip
> Sometimes the fabric looks a little loose on the Style-Vil. This is easy to fix with a water mister if you haven't pre-shrunk the fabric. Simply mist it and it will shrink slightly and fit the foam perfectly. You heard it here first!

METAL WORK

A bag will look 'homemade' rather than 'handmade' without professional-looking hardware. The great news is that it is inexpensive, found everywhere and easy to use – so much so that you feel a sense of achievement when you see what it does to a bag!

Rings can be 'D' or 'O' shaped or they can be rectangular. There is no difference at all apart from styling. Having said that, I tend to prefer the rectangular ones because the strap sits better on those with no gathering around the D curve. Sometimes a handle or a strap should be detachable to give you more options. Enter the trigger clasp! This little thingy (sorry about the technical language) means that you can decide whether your bag is a clutch or a tote. Cheap as chips and, like all of the metal hardware, it is available in several sizes and colours.

Then we have bag sliders. This is the tricksy little gizmo that is used on a long handle to make it adjustable (more about that in the techniques section). You will be given specifics in each pattern as to the size and then match the size of the strap or handle. You can get these in plastic or metal but I generally go for metal. I think that it looks better but it really depends on what you are doing.

Rivets are one of those things that make your bags look very professional. You need a special metal tool to insert them properly and I cannot stress enough that you should practise on a piece of cloth before approaching your bag! They require you to make a hole in the fabric and once you have done this, there really is no going back. Bear in mind that the shanks come in different lengths and you don't want one with a long shank for only two pieces of fabric, so when you buy them, check the shank length as well as the head size.

Plastic snap fasteners come in all sorts of colours. You can coordinate them with your fabrics and they are a great, simple and cheap way of closing a pocket or the top of a bag. They come with their own tool too; basically the snaps stay on because the tool squashes the shank from one half of the snap set into the middle of the corresponding piece.

Magnetic snaps are the grown-up cousins of the plastic snap fasteners. Whereas plastic snap fasteners are cheap and cheerful, the magnetic ones are sophisticated, strong and once again make your projects look lush. Putting them on is very easy and I would have a look online for a surgical scalpel and some blades – I don't need to tell you that these are super sharp and actually designed to cut flesh, do I...? But they are also super accurate and great for cutting through multiple layers of fabrics and interfacings.

Twist locks are another cannot-possibly-live-without item for your shopping list. They come in a couple of sizes and here again, I find a surgical scalpel perfect. I use a Swann-Morton #3 and a size 15 blade. My handle is left over from my days as a biologist and it has seen some action! I am very pleased to be able to continue using it for bag making. Your twist lock is one of those things that will help to make your bag look professionally handmade. (See pages 14–15 for fitting instructions for magnetic snaps and twist fasteners.)

13

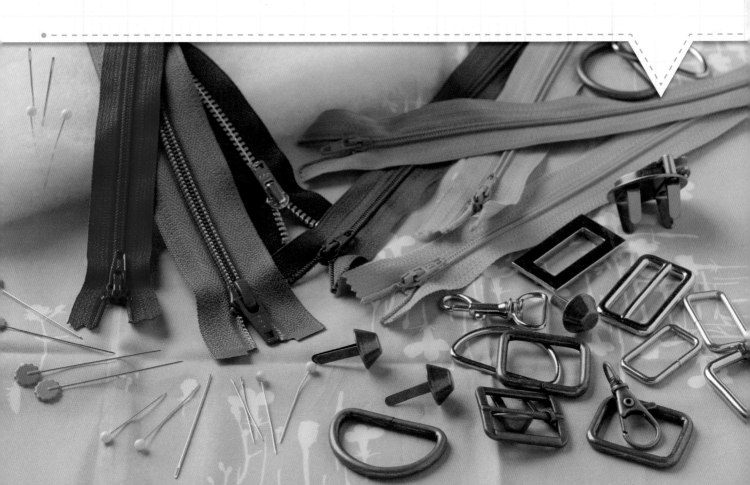

INSTALLING A MAGNETIC SNAP

1. Begin by identifying the area where you want your snap to sit. Cut a small square of fusible interfacing (such as Decovil or S320) – about 5cm (2in) square is perfect – and fuse this to the wrong side of where the snap is going. This will add a bit of reinforcement – these snaps actually do pull a little and with repeated opening and closing can show strain on delicate fabrics.

2. Mark the position of the magnetic snap with your water-soluble marker on the right side of the fabric.

3. Open the tines on the snap carefully and make sure that they are straight. Push them down over the marks and make little dents on the fabric.

4. Cut two tiny slits (too small is way better than too large) with the scalpel where you see the dents in the fabric.

5. Push the tines through.

6. On the back, put the plate onto the snap. Bend the tines outwards. There is some debate about in or out with this, but out creates less bulk so it's an easy choice for me!

7. Consider ironing a bit of fusible fleece (such as H630 or similar) over the back, because the tines are a little sharp and can wear the fabric over time. It feels nicer when you put your hand into the bag too.

8. Repeat for the other half of the snap.

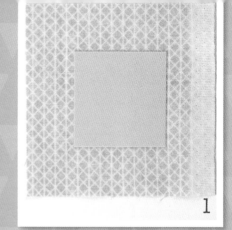

14

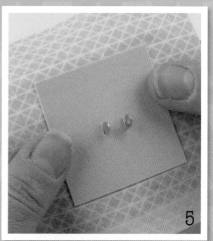

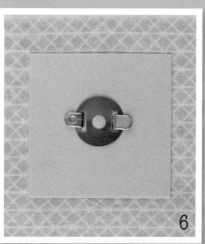

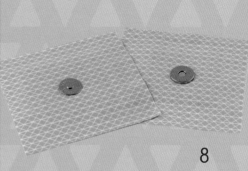

INSTALLING A TWIST FASTENER

Half of the lock (the male half; see tip box right) is installed in exactly the same way as a magnetic snap (see page 14) – it has tines and a little plate on the back to keep it in place. The other half will need some practice and you would do well to have a go on something not so precious as an almost complete bag... don't ask me how I know this!

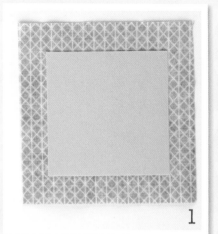

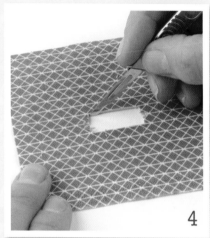

Tip

As non-PC as it sounds, locks traditionally have 'male' and 'female' parts, and it is fairly obvious which is which! Generally, the male bit goes into the female bit (sorry if this is a bit awful) – this is the same with everything from plastic snap fasteners to a sew-on button!

15

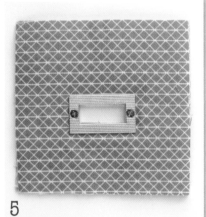

1. Decide where the female half of the lock will go. Cut a 5cm (2in) square of fusible interfacing (such as Decovil or S320) and fuse this to the wrong side of the fabric.

2. Use the water-soluble marker to draw around the inner rectangle bit of the lock and the two side bits where the screws go.

3. Press this down onto the fabric to mark it, then draw over the lines again with water-soluble marker.

4. Now cut out carefully, using a scalpel and cutting mat. Keep checking for fit and cut more as needed – the golden rule is that it is better to be too small because a smaller fit is tighter and more resilient, and you can always trim more away.

5. Place the front onto the front and the backing plate onto the back and screw it in, making sure that it is dead straight.

EQUIPMENT

Most of the things in this section will already be in your sewing box but a couple may not, so here I will explain why you cannot live without them any longer!

NEEDLES

No sewist worth the title will be without these. Even dedicated avoid-hand-sewing-at-all-costs people occasionally have to close a seam and do small jobs where the machine just will not do. I am not that fussy about which type of needle to use; aim for a medium-sized needle, which is not too thick and has an eye that you can see. Hand sewing usually comes in the form of sewing on buttons.

SCISSORS

We all know that you must keep your scissors *only* for fabric and I am going to repeat it here because it is important. If your significant other uses them to cut something in the kitchen or shed, it is actually grounds for divorce! They must be kept for fabric only. I also have a smaller pair, which are useful for snipping threads, and I have an older, less important pair for cutting other things such as paper and webbing straps.

DOUBLE-SIDED TAPE

This is a new one for most sewists but just as catwalk people use it to keep – um – bits and pieces of models inside clothes, it is also a great thing to use in bag making: keep a zip from moving around without pins to get in the way; close a strap before sewing and keep it all in place without pins to get in the way; position a patch pocket before sewing without pins to get in the way – the more astute amongst you will be seeing a pattern about now.

Double-sided tape is great for making things stay put and it lends an extra bit of rigidity too. I have two sizes: 1/4-inch (5mm) and 1/2-inch (1cm). The half is great for straps and the quarter is the only thing that stops me from going mad when putting in zips. Buy both in quantity.

WATER-SOLUBLE MARKERS

These are used a lot in sewing and quilting to make marks that can later on be removed with plain, cold water (I have a mister bottle and I use that). You can mark fabric, sew what is needed and then remove the ink. I have found though that for some reason, red fabric tends to be harder to remove them from. You can keep older ones for this though and because the ink is fainter, it is easier to remove.

One caveat, however; NEVER iron over them. Heat will set the ink in some fabric (you get to guess which) and then you will have a permanent mark – which is the opposite of ideal. Don't mark the fabric up and then get back to the project in six months either. Time can set the ink too. Mark as you need to and then get on with the job.

GLUE STICKS

Another surprise for a lot of people (although trust me, I am going to get even more surprising): don't spend an awful lot of money on 'fabric' glue sticks. The one from the office stores are the same glue and they do the same job.

Glue sticks give you another way of securing (and slightly stiffening, for that's really all fabric stiffener is too) something onto something else. I use a glue stick to keep a patch label in the right place while I sew around it (again, no pins). Glue sticks are helpful with the appliqué projects and you can apply them to very tiny pieces of fabric indeed. They will also make your life easier when it comes to layering up felt embellishments. Buy a glue stick.

HOT GLUE GUN

This one is not such a surprise. A hot glue gun is great for fixing mesh bag bases into the bottoms of bags and then putting the wadding/batting over the top. Things stay put, which is what you need really.

SEWING MACHINE

Don't write this one off as so obvious that it doesn't need to be said. You need a sewing machine and it needs to be able to handle a few layers of fabric, and it needs to be able to quilt (with a dual feed or walking foot) and do some free-motion embroidery (with a darning foot).

All of the patterns in this book have been sewn on my beautiful Janome Horizon Memory Craft 8200 QCP. Most modern sewing machines can handle the sorts of things that you will find in the following pages and you can buy accessories for just about anything.

TECHNIQUES

SEAMING

When you first look at it, making a bag can seem a bit scary – you are making a practical and usable 3D object. However, just like making clothes or quilts or anything else, it begins very simply – sewing two pieces of fabric together. To begin with, make sure that you cut your pattern pieces very accurately with sharp scissors. Near enough is not good enough and it will show in the final product. Check your cutting to make sure that it is accurate. Transfer any important pattern markings from the pattern to the fabric. This is where your water-soluble marker comes into its own. Darts, for example, have to be accurate and they will be if you transfer them straight from the pattern.

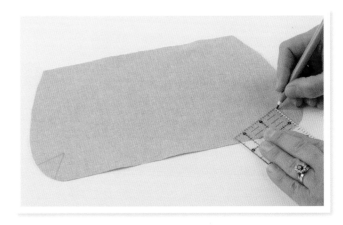

TO SEW TWO PIECES OF FABRIC TOGETHER

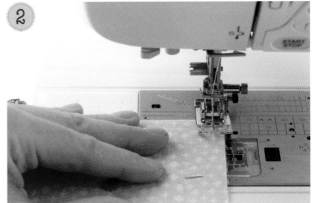

1. Place the two fabric pieces right sides together (the only time this will change is when you are French seaming, but this is not a technique used every day). Pin so that the pins run parallel to the top of the project. This will ensure that you can sew over them.

2. Place the two pieces onto the machine under the presser foot and lower the foot. You are after a 5mm (1/4in) seam and, in most cases, running the presser foot along the edge of the fabric will do this. This isn't foolproof though and every machine is different, so make a sample and measure yours. Then you will know where to sew each time without measuring the seam allowances.

3. Sew a couple of stitches and then reverse over them (back tack) to secure them. If you are working with a fine pattern piece and the fabric tends to get pushed down and puckers under the presser foot, shorten your stitch at the beginning and end instead. This helps to stop the stitches unravelling.

FINISHING SEAMS AND LINING

All of the projects in this book are lined so you don't have to worry about finishing seams. Lining is easy and it gives your bags a professional and well-made finish. I used three methods to line the bags in this book.

THE DROP-IN METHOD

Make your bag outer completely, finish it and have it the right way out. Do the same for the lining. With the wrong sides together this time, put the lining into the bag and then either turn the seam allowance in and sew around the top by hand, by machine topstitching or bind the edge (see page 20).

FOR NON-RIGID BAGS

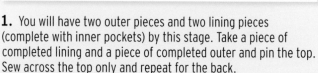

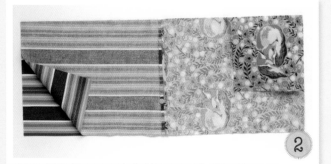

1. You will have two outer pieces and two lining pieces (complete with inner pockets) by this stage. Take a piece of completed lining and a piece of completed outer and pin the top. Sew across the top only and repeat for the back.

2. Open the pieces out and, with the right sides together, matching up the edges neatly, pin outer to outer and lining to lining.

3. Sew right around the outside leaving a gap in the lining large enough to turn the whole bag through.

4. Turn out through the gap and then close it either by hand or machine. Tuck the lining into the bag to complete.

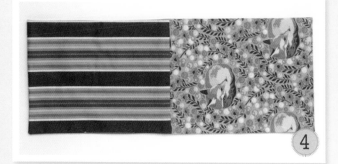

FOR STIFFER BAGS WITH A RIGID BOTTOM

1. Finish the bag outer and lining by adding any pockets and handles. With the right sides together, sew the outer around three sides (leaving the top edge open).

2. Sew the lining in the same way but leave a large enough gap in the side or bottom (whichever is the larger). Here, I marked my turning gap with pins before stitching to make life easier.

3. Turn the outer the right way out and the lining the wrong way out and slip the lining over the bag outer. The right sides should be together.

4. Match up seams and edges perfectly and pin around the top edge. Sew around the top edge.

5. Ease the bag out through the gap that you left and then close the gap.

6. Tuck the lining into the bag.

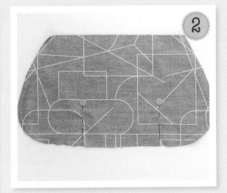

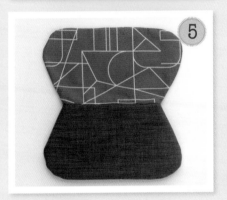

20

BINDING EDGES

Sometimes, when there is a lot going on with a bag and it is rigid or a funny shape or none of the methods above even comes close, the best way is to sew the pieces together and then bind the raw edge and make a feature of it. You can either hide the binding inside the bag or make it a real stand-out on the outside.

1. Trim the edges so that they are as neat as possible – sometimes they will have a lot of bulk. Choose your binding and sew it on by hand with neat, small stiches, beginning on the 'best' side.

2. Now come back and do the same on the other side, enclosing the raw edge in the binding. You can do this by machine but it is often very fiddly and not much quicker.

PATCHWORKING

Patchworking is essentially just sewing two pieces of fabric together, except this time the focus is on making patterns and special effects with the fabric. There are a couple of things to remember:

1. Cut accurately and this will make for accurate piecing.
2. It is alright to iron seams open – this will reduce bulk.
3. Iron at every stage of the proceedings.

The only patchworking that is slightly more tricky is used for the Margaret geometric bag, shown right and on pages 88–93. It uses isosceles triangles.

PATCHWORKING WITH TRIANGLES

Triangles are a bit more challenging than squares because you have to make sure that you leave a seam allowance at the top so that you do not ruin your points.

1. Begin with two accurate triangles and place them right sides together. Remember that one has to be upside down in order to form a straight line. Align them so that they fit together with a small amount of overhang on the top and bottom.

2. Start sewing at the top edge and sew the seam.

3. Open out and press.

4. Add another triangle and repeat until you have enough on the row.

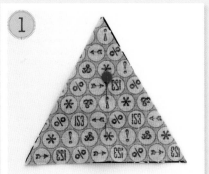

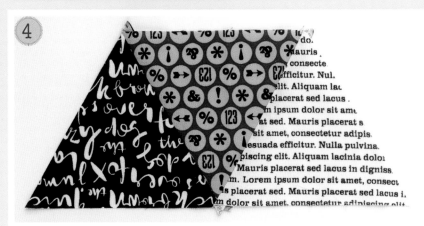

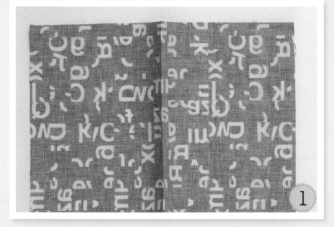

INSERTING A ZIP

Zips aren't scary. You'll need a zip foot for your machine and a small amount of practice, but then you will be confident enough to put them into everything!

INSERTING A BOX ZIP POCKET

These zips look good anywhere on your bag – I often use them on the backs to make an extra pocket.

1. Begin by cutting an outer panel and then a lining panel according to the instructions in the pattern. Take the piece of lining destined to back the outer and crease it in half vertically to find the centre.

2. Turn the lining piece to the wrong side and on one short end (it doesn't matter which) measure down from the top and make a mark. The individual pattern will tell you how far to measure. Measure your zip from stop to stop, NOT from the end of the tape to the end of the tape. In this case, it is 18cm (7in) so my box needs to be drawn 18 x 1cm (7 x $^3/_8$in). Using a water-soluble marker, draw this box onto the wrong side of the lining. This is the sewing line.

3. Draw a second line across the middle with angled lines at the ends. This is the cutting line, but don't cut just yet.

4. Place the outer panel right sides together with your lining piece and pin together. Sew around the outer box shape.

5. Cut along the cutting line. Be very careful not to cut through the stitches.

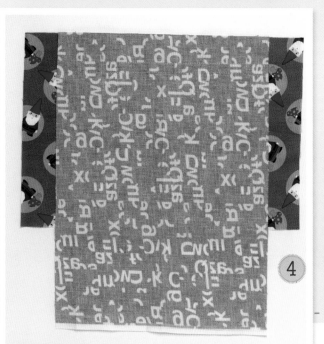

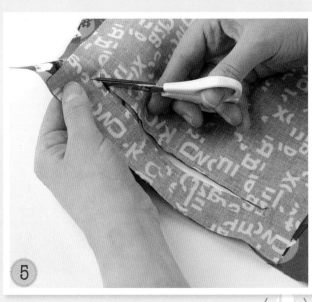

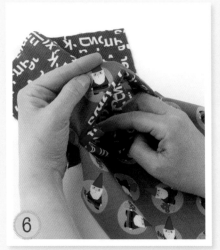

6. 'Post' the lining through the hole.

7. Smooth it out perfectly and press. A fine mist of water is very valuable here (better than steam, I find).

8. Sew the zip tape ends together on the opening end. This makes a smoother result. Using narrow double-sided tape, prepare your zip by sticking a length either side of the zip teeth, on the right side of the zip.

9. Stick the zip on the lining side of the hole, making sure that it lines up as perfectly as possible.

10. Topstitch around the box to secure the zip.

11. Bring the long piece of lining up and align the top edge. Sew the sides together and the top edge in place – be very careful here: do not sew the sides to the outer piece of fabric. Sometimes, if there isn't much room (in a purse for example) you will have only a bare minimum of seam allowance to sew. Use a zip foot to do the job instead.

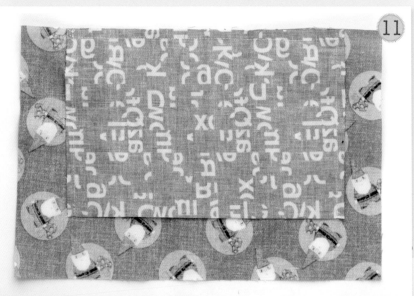

INSERTING A BOX TOP ZIP

The other sort of zip used in this book is a box top zip. It uses more pieces of fabric but isn't very difficult to achieve either. For this technique, imagine you are making a 'zip sandwich'!

1. Take your zip and two rectangles of fabric, one outer and one lining (the sizes will be given in the pattern). Pin one of the outer rectangles right sides together to one side of your zip.

2. Tack/baste along this line and then sew on your machine; remove the tacking/basting stitches. Put the lining on, right sides together with the first piece – the zip will be in between the two to make the 'sandwich'. Sew the seam.

3. Open the rectangles out and then topstitch along the edge of the teeth to ensure the fabrics lie flat. Repeat for the other side of the zip.

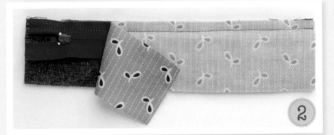

Tip

As you sew you will need to move the zip head out of the way to avoid creating a 'wiggle' in your stitches if you try to sew around it. Leave the needle in the fabric and simply open or close the zip to move it out of the way when you come to it.

MAKING BOX CORNERS

Making a box corner gives a bag more volume, creating a dimensional object with a shape to it rather than a flat item. It also allows you to add reinforcement to the bottom of the bag, if relevant, in the form of interfacing, mesh or even foam board. The good news is that it is not at all difficult to do. There are a couple of ways of achieving a box corner and I have chosen my favourite (and the one used in this book!) to share with you. This method is easiest when dealing with layers and it allows you to see exactly where the seam is.

The pattern will tell you when to box the corner, and by how much. It is done when the front and back of the bag are sewn together. Don't change this amount because it will have an impact on the rest of the bag. Always do exactly the same thing for the lining unless directed otherwise.

1. Transfer the box measurement to the wrong side of the bag with your water-soluble marker.

2. Cut the corner sections out.

3. Pinch the corner together so that the side and bottom seams are exactly on top of one another; pin. Make sure that there is no puckering on the right side of the fabric, especially where there are many layers.

4. Sew across the corner.

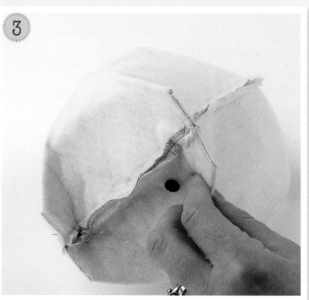

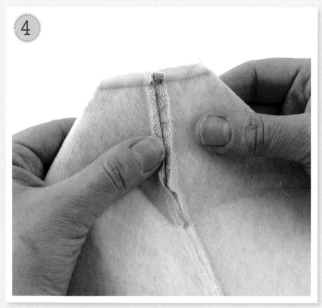

CLIPPING, NOTCHING AND CUTTING ACROSS CORNERS

Bag making means bulk. You add layers of interfacing, the fabric itself and then reinforce this and strengthen that. You can end up with nine or ten layers! This can result in clumsy edges and chunky points, and that is far from ideal. The solution is to trim judiciously and remove some of the excess.

CROSS-CORNER CUT

The first example is the simple cross-corner cut. You will have sewn the layers together around three sides resulting in something that looks like the image shown right. Then, with the piece still inside out, cut straight across the corners, being very careful not to cut the stitching (see far right). This simple act alone will mean that your corner has less bulk when turned through – it will be easier to make it into a sharp point.

CLIPPING

Sometimes, where there is much more bulk, you can come back a second time. By making two more cuts at an angle, more bulk is gone. Again, be super careful not to cut the stitches, and always leave a margin of fabric for the stitches to 'grip', especially on looser weaves, as the stitches can come undone if you cut too radically.

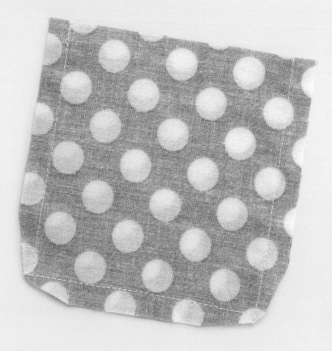

CUTTING NOTCHES

When you sew a curve such as a rounded flap, such as for Lorle on pages 48–51, or a tab, the finished product will not lie flat without some surgery beforehand. Once you have sewn the tab or flap (the principle is the same) and you are ready to turn it out the right way, cut little 'v' shapes with a small pair of sharp scissors all around the curve, being careful not to cut the stitching. When the tab or flap is turned out the right way and pressed, these little 'v' shapes will nestle together and without the extra fabric in between, you will avoid puckering.

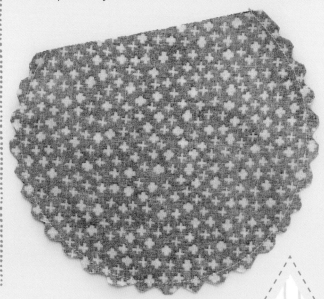

MAKING BIAS BINDING

You can buy bias binding and although it is not available in all colours, the range is quite wide and the quality is mostly good. I have used it in a couple of places in the following projects: see Tilde, page 65, or Ingrid, page 104. So why would you bother to make your own? In a word: choice. You can coordinate perfectly if you know how to make your own binding. And the same thing will be used for piping (see page 29) so it is very versatile. First, get yourself a bias strip maker. They come in four different sizes and they don't cost very much... plus you will be happy to avoid burned fingers! So how do we begin?

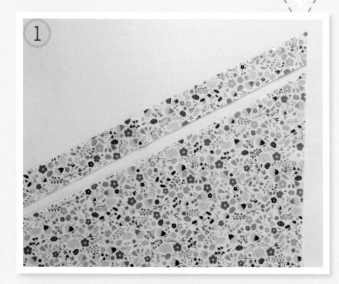

1. Cut strips on the bias. This means to cut diagonally across the grain and not with it. The reason for this is that a bias strip then has more 'give' and will sit neatly around a curve without puckering. My strips are usually 3.5cm (1³⁄₈in) wide.

2. Join the strips together. Take two strips and place them right sides together. Allow a little 'ear' to protrude each side (don't match them exactly or they will be off kilter when you open them out). Sew across the strip.

3. Keep going until you have enough length. The pieces will stretch slightly, but cut and measure so that you know that you have plenty for your project.

4. Push the end of the strip into the bias tape maker. Pull on the handle of the bias tape maker as you iron the bit coming out of the other end. The bias maker will fold the tape for you.

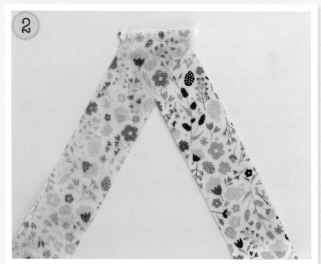

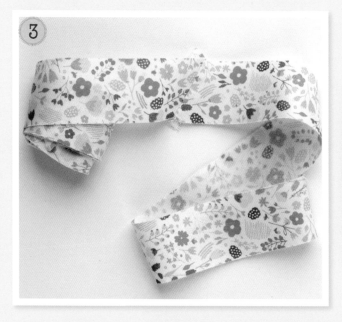

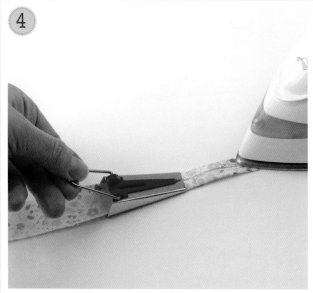

APPLYING BIAS BINDING

You can put bias binding on completely by hand and also completely by machine. The first way is slower but the second way tends not to be as neat as I like it to be, so I use a combination of the two.

1. To bind an edge, open out your tape and lay it on the edge of the bag part to be bound. You are working on the right side (brown) of the project. Pin.

2. Sew along the tape using the crease as a guide.

3. Fold the tape over the raw edge. The centre crease is a really useful guide to show whether your tape is straight along the edge. Pin in place, with the raw edge tucked under and covering your machine stitches from step 2.

4. Stitch with a small ladder stitch along the wrong side (blue trees) of the project to secure the back of the tape.

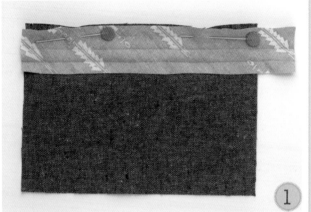

STRAIGHT BINDING

And what about straight binding? Straight binding is the same thing as bias binding except that it is cut on the straight grain. It measures the same width and the length will be in the pattern. You can use this where there are no curves to negotiate, such as along the tops of pockets. The advantage is that it uses slightly less fabric and there is no stretch, so if the rest of the pocket is bias-cut, the straight binding can help to give it structure.

PIPING

Piping – either round or flat – makes a great impact and adds a professional touch to your bag making. It can be made in a contrasting colour or it can be made from the same colour or print as a textural detail.

The great news is that if you can make bias binding, you are halfway there. Have a look at page 27 and to make piping, just follow the bias binding steps 1–3. Once you have enough continuous binding strip, rather than put it through a bias tape maker, simply fold it in half lengthways. Don't iron it though, because we don't want a crease, just a soft fold. From here, you have two choices. You can apply it to a bag section as it is, or you can insert piping cord in the middle to give more structure – see below.

TO MAKE PIPING CORD

Piping cord will make your flat piping rounded and more structured. Here again, you start off with bias binding – 3.5cm (1³⁄₈in) wide is a versatile size.

1. Fold the bias binding over but don't iron it.

2. Tuck the piping cord into it, close the fold and pin.

3. Sew along the length as close to the piping cord as you can. You will need your zip foot to make this perfect.

TO APPLY PIPING

1. Take the two sections to be piped and place one piece down with the right side up.

2. Place the piping onto it with the raw edges facing the outer edge of the fabric. Place the second piece of fabric on the top, right side down. Pin.

3. Sew along the edge, enclosing the piping.

4. Open or turn the pieces out the right way and press carefully.

Depending on where the piping is, you can then topstitch to make the layers behave, or, if it is on a pocket or edge, nothing more needs to be done. The structure of the bag will hold everything in place.

30

INSERTING PATCH POCKETS

We all need more storage and these bags are full of little compartments to put things in. Never waste the inside of a bag – that is an opportunity to add at least two patch pockets. These are so easy to make and the lined ones are really the business. Don't leave out the interfacing. It adds a special something and makes the pocket look so much crisper.

1. Begin by cutting the fusible interfacing (I mainly use S320 for this job as it is rigid enough but has some flexibility). In the patterns, the sizing is always for the interfacing and we build the fabric around that. Cut two more pieces of fabric, one of the chosen outer for the pocket and one for the lining. These have to be 1cm ($^3/_8$in) larger all around than the interfacing. Fuse the interfacing to the wrong side of the outer fabric.

2. Lay the fused outer fabric right sides together with the lining and pin. Sew around the very edge of the interfacing, using it as a guide. Leave a turning gap in the bottom edge.

3. Trim the seam allowance back to a 'normal' 5mm ($^1/_4$in) width and then clip across the corners.

4. Turn out through the gap and press so that the edges are perfect. The lining should not be visible from the front. The pocket is now ready to use.

31

Tip

A wooden chopstick is perfect for gently persuading the corners to be sharp and beautiful. Go easy though – one slightly overzealous push and you will be through the stitching!

5. A double patch pocket uses the same method except for the fact that you make two patch pockets, one slightly smaller than the other.

6. After they have been turned through and pressed, sew the smaller pocket over the larger one with a narrow seam and from then on treat them as one piece.

7. Sometimes a pocket is too generous and needs some subdivisions – if they are too big, they can gape. To make a section or two in a pocket, simply mark a vertical line where you want it to be and sew straight up.

STRAPS, HANDLES AND TABS

Not every bag is a clutch or a purse. Sometimes, you want something to hang on to! Just like bias binding, you can buy handles readymade and sometimes we use webbing or similar to get the job done. Mostly though, you'll want to make straps and handles that coordinate with your bags so that you can control how they look. There are several different types of handle and we will go through them one by one: thin ones, thicker ones, folded ones and adjustable ones.

DETACHABLE STRAPS

You can see a detachable strap with a trigger clip on the Lorle purse on pages 48–51. This is an example of a thinner strap. The pattern will give you the specifics but do check on a measuring tape and if your hand is very small or a little larger, you may need to subtract or add some centimetres to the length.

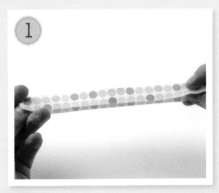
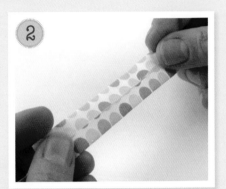

   A strap like this one needs hardware too, which is 'built in' as you sew. The strap is made from a piece of fabric that is four times the desired finished width. It has no interfacing and the fabric folds support it and give it strength. Thicker straps will be looked at on page 33.

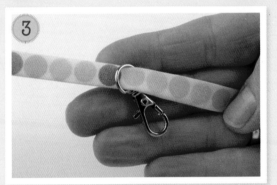
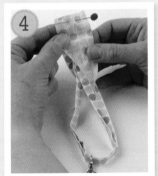

32

1. Cut the strap size from your chosen fabric, as per your project instructions, and fold in half lengthways. Iron.

2. Fold the two raw edges in to the centre crease and iron them too.

3. Thread on your trigger clip.

4. With the right sides together, sew the end closed (just move the clip out of the way). This will upset the folds a bit but you can finger press them back in.

5. Refold the strap and secure with some thin double-sided tape. This is better than pins, which get in the way, plus it can stay in the strap – it will provide a bit of structure too.

6. Sliding the clip along as you go, topstitch both sides of the strap.

7. Find the end and put the clip next to it; keep it there with a rivet.

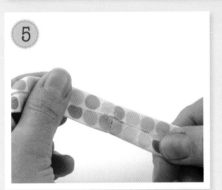
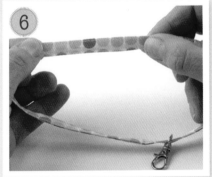

TABS

A tab is happily very similar to a strap. Complete steps 1 and 2 and then go straight to step 6 and topstitch both sides of the strap (see opposite). This can then be cut to any length and used to make a decoration, or to house the 'D'-ring to attach a detachable strap. You can use them to add an embellishment, too, so they are super handy.

Tabs will almost always echo the width of the strap. The detachable strap has a corresponding small tab and a wider strap will be the same. To save time and effort, the patterns often instruct you to make a longer handle strap and then cut a certain amount off the end of it to use for tabs. That way, the size is uniform.

OPEN-ENDED STRAPS

Most of the projects in this book have straps that are open-ended. This means that they have raw ends that are designed to be hidden inside the seam of a bag, or to be folded over and stitched to form an adjustable handle, as for a cross-body purse or a backpack (see page 34). Once again, you can play with the lengths. I like to put a tote on my shoulder because I hate carrying things if I don't have to. Hands-free all the way! So check the length of straps suggested in the pattern and adapt them as necessary.

These straps are a lot wider than the detachable strap featured opposite. To begin with, your wider strap will need interfacing of some sort – the exact amounts will be given in the pattern. I use one main sort of interfacing for straps and (keep this a secret) it isn't actually designed for strap making! It is called Bundfix tape and its original use is for waistbands on trousers and skirts. But actually, it is fabulous for making very quick and very accurate straps and handles! The best thing about it is that, depending on how you fold it, you can achieve a couple of different strap widths! It has handy perforations along the way for accurate folding too. I used a tape width of 7cm (2³/₄in) throughout.

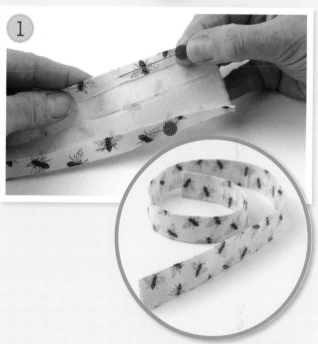

OPTION 1

Begin with the length of tape that you need and then cut it – the pattern will tell you, but if you are smaller or larger, please feel free to lengthen or shorten this. Cut the fabric that you have chosen for the strap and join if needed to get the length. Fuse the tape to the wrong side. Now here we have a few variations. For a 2.5cm (1in) finished strap, cut the fabric exactly the same width as the tape. Fold in half and fold the raw edges to the centre; topstitch along both edges.

OPTION 2

For a slightly wider strap (3.5cm/1³/₈in finished) cut the fabric 10cm (4in) wide and then fold it over the tape edge rather than at the outer perforations as you did before. Now fold in half at the centre using the perforations as a guide. Topstitch along both edges, then sew the width of the presser foot in from that to create four lines of stitching.

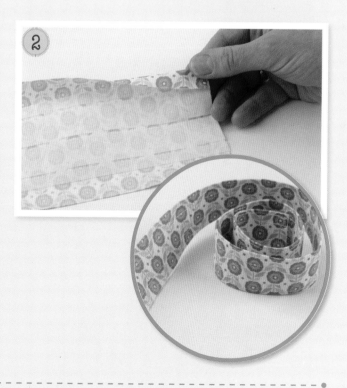

FITTING ADJUSTABLE STRAPS

Nothing makes you feel more like a boss than fitting an adjustable strap. I know – small victories – but try it and tell me then that I am overreacting! You will fit one of these to an adjustable bag like Claudia on pages 70–73 or even two as you see on the Minna backpack on pages 78–83.

You will need a bag slider that is just a tiny bit larger than your strap; the pattern will give you the details. You will also need two 'D'-rings – these will be attached to the bag using tabs that are the same size as your strap. By the time you come to attach the strap, your tabs and 'D'-rings will already be attached to your bag.

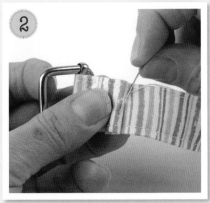

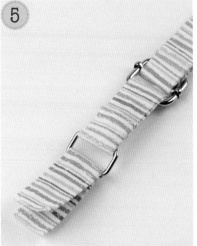

1. Start with your open-ended strap. Thread it through the centre bar of the bag slider.

2. Fold it over and stitch either by hand or machine. I actually prefer hand stitching because it is easier to get in close. You can add a rivet too if you like.

3. Take the other end of the strap and thread it though one of the 'D'-rings on the bag.

4. Now take the strap back through the bag slider.

5. Go to the other 'D'-ring and attach the end of the strap the same way that you did on the middle bar of the bag slider in step 2.

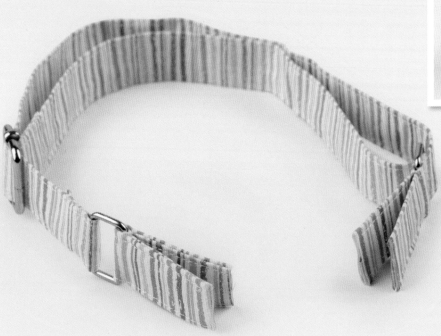

EMBELLISHMENT

Without embellishments, bags are just bags. The embellishments give them their character and bring them alive. There are so many ways that you can add a special something to a bag – embroidery, appliqué and charms name only a few and all of these plus a few more will be looked at in the next pages. The great thing about embellishments is that, like colour and fabric, they allow you to change the look of a bag. If you love a bag shape but think that the embellishment on another one would look better, there is nothing stopping you from changing it. An embellishment doesn't change the structure of a bag so feel free to swap to your heart's content.

EMBROIDERY

There is a whole world of embroidery out there – this book will give you a taster and show you some simple steps. Embroidery though, much like maths, is actually built on some really simple concepts, so once you have the basics you can go on as you like. All of the designs in this book use one or two of the following stitches: straight stitch, running stitch, backstitch, lazy daisy, chain stitch and French knot. Let's start at the beginning with a straight stitch.

STRAIGHT STITCH

To make this simplest of all stitches start by threading your needle with embroidery floss. The pattern will always tell you how many strands to use. Knot one end and then you're off! See the radiating straight stitches I used on Hannah, shown right and on pages 66–69.

1. Bring the needle up from the back of the fabric at A.

2. Take it down again somewhere on your design (B) – here again, the pattern will tell you and there will be a template to follow if you want it.

3. Keep coming up and going down until the design is filled with colour.

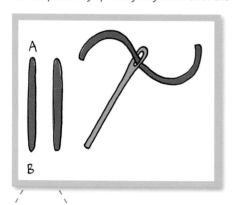

RUNNING STITCH

Next in the category of easier-than-falling-off-a-log embroidery is running stitch. I used it to outline elements of Lotte, see below left and pages 74–77 or Gertrude, below right and pages 112–115.

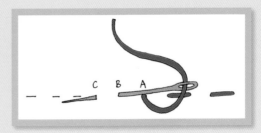

1. Bring the knotted thread up somewhere on the design (A).

2. Instead of going down again as in a straight stitch, go up and down through the fabric a few times with a rocking motion and then pull the needle. This way you will get a few running stitches at once (B–C).

3. Keep going! The only thing to remember with a running stitch is that essentially, you are free handing. This stitch is most used to quilt things (the old way was always running stitch) and it is also used to make borders and things like that. If you don't watch the stitches, they can get larger or smaller over time and you will have to unpick and start again.

BACKSTITCH

This is what running stitch and straight stitch would do if they got their act together. It is essentially a way to outline and make a statement with an unbroken line. It has a starring role in embroidery for stems, outlines and lettering. I didn't actually use it on any of these bags, but no stitch guide would be complete without it – so you can have this one for free!

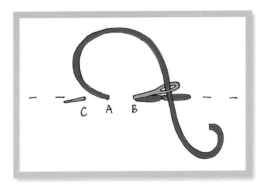

1. Begin once again with your needle threaded and come up from the back of the work at A.

2. Go down at B which, as you can see from the line, is behind A. This is the 'back' bit of backstitch.

3. Come back up at point C. Go back down again at A, in the same hole so that you get your unbroken line.

4. Continue until you have the line that you want.

5. Because you have to determine the lengths of the stitches as you go, make sure that you keep checking to see that they are not getting longer and longer.

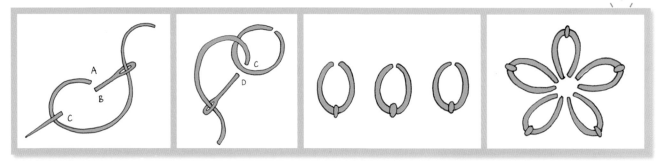

LAZY DAISY STITCH

Flowers! This stitch is all about making little flower and folkloric comma-like embellishments on your work. It is also known as a broken or detached chain stitch. Once you get going with it, you will be able to make the prettiest flowers and little blossoms, and they are fun to scatter across your work. See Lorle, right and pages 48–51, or Sylvia, below right and pages 120–123.

1. Bring the thread up from the back of the work (A) and then take the needle back to where you came up, as close as possible to the thread (B).

2. The needle will be quite flat on the work at this point. Loop the thread around the point of the needle.

3. Hold the loop stable with a thumb and then gently pull the thread until it is taut.

4. Finish the stitch with a tiny anchor at the end of the loop (C–D).

5. Make a flower by making another four of these little stitches with the pointy ends in the middle. Don't come up through the same hole to make each one though; allow a bit of room for a French knot centre.

CHAIN STITCH

This is essentially the same deal as the detached chain that we just looked at to make a flower. It is a handy stitch that creates a line that is a little more dramatic than a backstitch. It is also great for borders.

1. Start as though you were making a lazy daisy stitch.

2. When you get to the anchor stitch bit, instead of making a tiny stitch just to hold the loop, come up again at C with the flat needle and make another lazy daisy stitch.

3. Keep going until you have a chain.

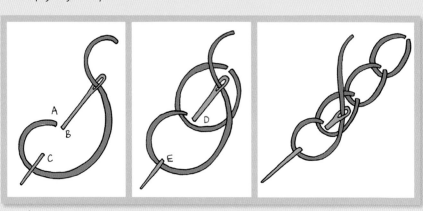

FRENCH KNOT

The centres of flowers and little dots are usually made with a French knot. It is a basic stitch but very useful. You can use just one in a flower centre or dozens all packed in together to cover the fabric. See Lorle, below and on pages 48–51 – here I used yellow French knots for the flower centres and scattered orange French knots around for decoration.

1. Begin by bringing the thread up from the back of the work at A.

2. Wrap the thread around the needle about three times (changing the number of wraps will change the size of your knot, so practise to see what looks good).

3. Slide your wraps down the thread to make a knot.

4. Take the needle back down near to where you came up, at B, leaving a little knot behind on the fabric surface.

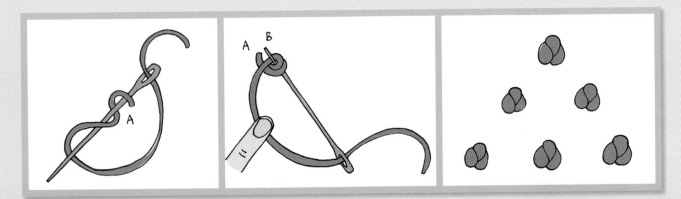

APPLIQUÉ

Another wonderful way to add interest and character is through appliqué. Appliqué has been with us for a very long time and every now and then it goes through an identity reboot and a renaissance. Right now, it is all about raggy-edge appliqué. As luck would have it, raggy-edge appliqué is one of the easiest to do. Unlike needle turn, there is no fiddly hand sewing and fear of fraying the edges too far – instead, you want the edges to fray!

Raggy-edge appliqué is teamed with free-motion embroidery (FME), and the very close stitches of FME mean that the frayed edges do not travel far and spoil your work. Even after washing. Happy days! We will discuss these two techniques together over the next few pages. FME can stand alone as a machine doodling technique that you can use for writing and embellishment, but raggy-edge appliqué really needs its support. The two examples shown right give you an idea of what sorts of things can be done.

TEMPLATES

In any pattern with appliqué you will have a template. In my patterns, where the templates are layered to get an effect, I will show you which bit is behind another with a dotted line. This means that you can see the overall shape and then you can see which bit is behind and by how much.

You will need your trusty water-soluble marker for appliqué and it is quite often a good idea to make either a thin plastic or card template from your patterns. You can reuse the template this way, and if it is a heart or a flower, you can just bet that you will want it again. Cereal-box card makes a good template if you are on a budget and you can laminate it with old-fashioned contact paper. When you have a template, you just need to trace around it with your water-soluble marker and cut it out with a sharp pair of scissors. We discussed glue before but let's revisit here. Use your glue stick to layer the pieces so that when you sew you don't have to fuss with pins or bother about things shifting too much. The glue will not give you a solid hold – so still be careful – but it is a lot easier.

FABRICS

You can use any sort of non-stretchy fabric for appliqué. The most commonly used ones in this book are cottons and felts. You can get great effects from the two of these.

SO WHAT ABOUT FME?

Good question. FME is what keeps it all together, and most modern sewing machines can manage it no problem at all. There are a couple of things to know though: you either have to be able to drop the feed dogs (that metal plate with the 'teeth' on it under your needle) or set your stitch length to zero. The reason for this is that when you are doing FME you are aiming to sew curves and allow the fabric layers to move fluidly through the machine. The feed dogs want to pull it straight through. By disabling them or setting a zero stitch length, you have to pull the fabric through and, with practice, you can write and doodle and do all sorts of things. The other thing that you will need is a darning foot (see below). This allows you a free range of movement with your doodling and won't fight to keep on the straight and narrow the way a normal presser foot will.

PUTTING IT ALL TOGETHER

So you have followed your pattern and built a simple appliqué shape, for example, an apple, as shown below right. You have an apple shape and a crescent piece for a shiny reflection. Here's what you do:

1. Apply glue to the shapes and position them where you want them. Run over the shapes with an iron to dry the glue and then they will stay put. If you are not happy with the placement, peel them off, apply more glue and then re-iron.

2. Set your machine up for FME; consult your manual or the manufacturer's website if you need to.

3. Choose a colour of thread that will either complement your fabric or really stand out. Black can look great with florals, depending on the look that you are going for. Experiment and think outside the box.

4. Put the same colour into the bobbin for a clear line or choose a different bobbin colour for a denim mélange effect.

5. Place your piece of work onto the machine bed, lower the needle and start doodling the outline. FME looks good if you go over it twice here and there and don't aim to be super neat. That's the whole point of it.

6. I would do a single line on small pieces and a double on the larger bits – this is a bit of a get-out-of-jail-free card too because you can correct mistakes. If your line goes a bit wonky and close to the edge, go around again and make it wonky all the way around. That way it looks deliberate! Go slow and concentrate. Now is not the time to be looking at the television. This stitching is really close together. That is both a good and a bad thing. Good because it limits the fraying and bad because it is virtually impossible to unpick. Work slowly and deliberately and watch what you are doing.

7. Use your water-soluble pen to draw in the stalk and leaf, and then stitch over these in the same way.

8. When you have finished, snip the threads away from the front and back to complete.

CROCHETED FLOWERS

Crochet is an easy thing to learn if it is not a skill that you have already and there are some very good books and online tutorials to help you get started. I will assume that you have the basics and, with those basics, I want to show you how to make a little flower that is super useful to brighten up a bag or to just add that special something. Before we begin, let me tell you that I am fairly new to crochet and no virtuoso – so if I can do it, it must be really simple!

I am using a fingering (4-ply) yarn in 100% mercerised cotton, which has a bit of a sheen. Use a 4mm (UK 8, US G/6) hook – the larger the hook, the more 'open' your work will be (bigger holes) and that is not ideal.

1. Make a slip knot.

2. Ch 4, join the chain into a circle with a sl st.

3. Ch 3 (counts as first tr).

4. 9 tr into the ring, sl st into the top of the first ch to close the loop (10 sts).

5. There are spaces between each of the tr sts. Make 5 tr in the first space (this makes a pretty scalloped petal).

6. *Sl st into the next space and then 5 tr in the next space, rep from * until you have five petals.

7. Fasten off, weave in the ends and decorate the centre of the flower with a pretty button.

By the way, if you want to make a six-petal flower, make 11 tr instead of 9 tr in step 4. To make a double flower, simply make two and sew them together. They can be the same colour, or totally different depending on the look that you are going for.

ADAPTING CHARMS TO MAKE BROOCHES

Every now and then, we want a change. Sometimes the change that we are after is as simple as a new embellishment on a bag! The little flowers are really easy to adapt and they can be sewn into place using the button in the centre or you can glue them onto a brooch bar so that they can be swapped around a bit.

1. Go for a brooch back with a bit of surface area on it, such as a disc or similar.

2. Rub the disc a bit with ordinary sandpaper. This will provide something for the glue to bond with.

3. Hot glue the flower onto the brooch back. You're done!

42

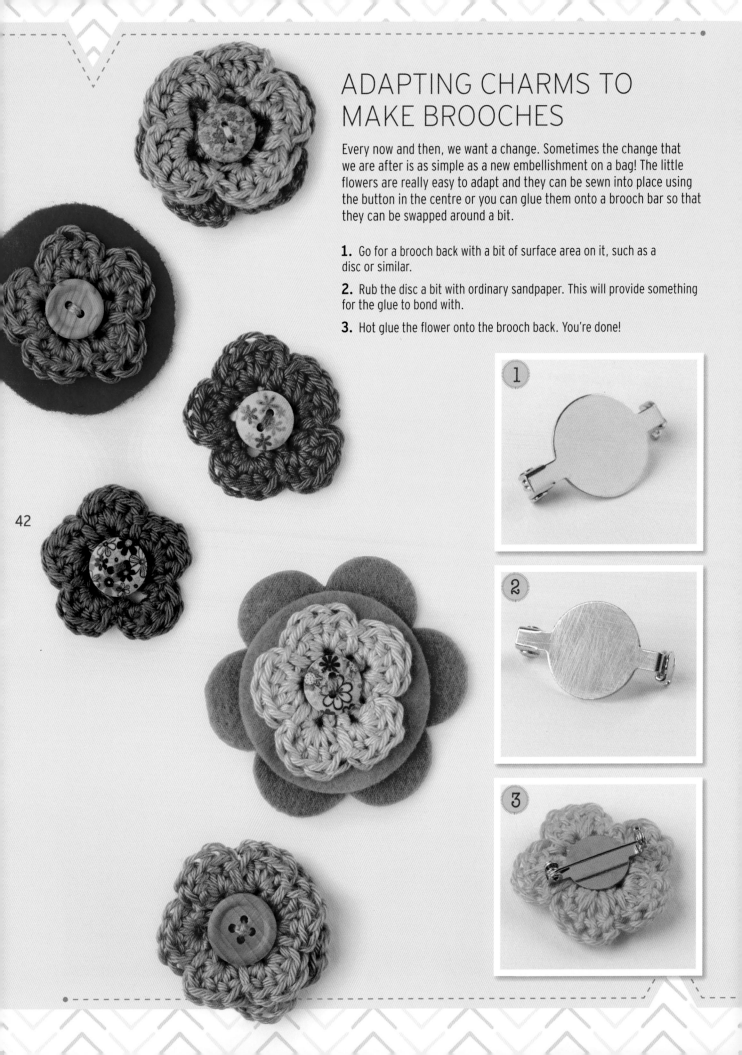

BEADED CHARMS

Every craft on the planet has its own arsenal of tools and requirements, as most crafters know. However, this is a book about sewing, so the good news is that I am not sending you down to the beading store with a long list!

My beaded charms only need a needle small enough to pass through the beads and some thread. Oh, and some beads! But they are fun things and they don't count as purchases at the craft store... The thing about beaded charms is that they need to be strong. You don't want to hear the delicate ping of beads scooting and bouncing across the floor at any time. To make sure that they are strong, I like to pass the thread up and down through the beads and around the top anchor point (usually a zip pull) a few times. You will need to buy beads of a few sizes and you will need the odd trigger clip, and that's about it.

TO MAKE A BASIC CHARM

1. Thread your needle with quite a long piece of thread. Fold it double. The needle has to be small enough to pass through the bead centre but the eye has to be large enough to take four lots of thread as you will see in a second. Choose an anchor bead and thread it on. I like a small silver one for this job as a rule.

2. Now cut the thread off close to the needle, centre the anchor bead in the middle of it and rethread the needle – this is what I was talking about before.

3. Now make a bead 'kebab' by choosing the beads that will suit your project and threading them on. Don't make it too long – keep looking and checking that it looks right for the application. Choose your anchor point: here I used a trigger clip, but it could be a zip pull too (see right) or even a 'D'-ring put onto the bag for just this purpose. Thread the needle twice around through the ring on the bottom.

4. Now go back through the beads. And then back around the ring, and back through the beads and keep doing this until the thread cannot go through any more. Fasten off and bury any knots in the nearest bead.

See! No special equipment needed and no special beading skills needed either. But don't underestimate the value of putting these here and there on bags for maximum impact!

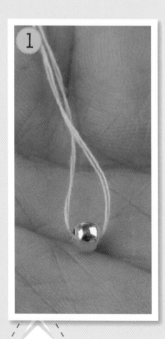

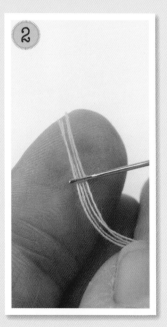

MAKING LABELS

Now I know that you are not the sort of person who buys something just for the label(!) but labels are nice all the same and have a really important place in the world of design. A label can be your identifying mark or it can be just a simple scrap of lace peeking out of a side seam. My labels tend to reflect what the bag is trying to say rather than my official brand. I like to put a surprise label in a bag, inside a pocket or similar where it can wish you a good morning. These quirky little details are what will make your bags different and very individual. The best news is that they are quite simple to make. I make my labels with the following (very short I promise) list of needs:

1. Kraft-tex™ paper: this delightful leathery stuff comes on a roll and it behaves like fabric and paper combined. It can be washed and I use normal paper craft stamps to embellish it (see the bee label below and the horse label bottom right).

2. Cotton tape: in different widths and colours. This is great for a slightly rustic feel to a label. Invest in some liquid seam sealant though and treat the ends or watch your label unravel before your very eyes! (See opposite for treating the ends, and the flower, butterfly and bee labels, right.)

3. Stamps and ink: usually specialist equipment is required but in this case, that is not so. I use 'normal' paper craft stamps. My favourite ink is Ranger Archival™ in Jet Black. It doesn't run, it dries quickly and you can wash it. Save the stamps that come free with magazines (as a fabric crafter you may not do this). When buying, choose stamps that do not have a lot of fussy detail. You can get away with it on Kraft-tex™ paper but not on the cotton tape. Add some alphabet stamps to your kit in different sizes and then you can say anything that you want – perfect if the right stamp just doesn't exist.

44

HOW TO MAKE A LABEL

Labels can be long and thin; they can be short and fat. It depends on your needs at the time. They are super easy to make!

1. Roughly cut a piece of Kraft-tex™.

2. Choose your stamp and then use it.

3. Neaten the edges, remembering to leave enough room for stitching.

MAKING A TAPE LABEL

Similar to Kraft-tex™ but with a bit of prior prep.

1. Fix the ends with liquid seam sealant and allow plenty of room with this so that you can trim to the right length. Allow to dry.

2. Stamp using your chosen image or words.

3. Trim and sew into place.

 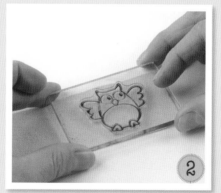 

The Bags

Lorle

I know bag makers are not all necessarily embroiderers, but when the stitches are this easy and the results this nice it is worth crossing over occasionally. This is a handy and summery purse that will make you feel as though the sun is shining even if, strictly speaking, it isn't.

Finished size: 17 x 12cm (6²/₃ x 4¾in), plus strap

Gather these supplies

Fabrics
- A: 1 fat eighth blue linen, for the flap
- B: 1 fat eighth red and white polka dot linen, for the front and back pieces and inner patch pocket
- C: 1 fat eighth green coordinating fabric, for lining and strap

Interfacings
- 1 fat sixteenth fusible woven interfacing (such as G740)
- 1 fat eighth fusible interfacing (such as S320)
- 1 fat eighth fusible wadding/batting (such as H640)
- Scrap of lightweight fusible interfacing (such as Decovil I Light)

Everything else
- 20cm (8in) coordinating woven ribbon
- Embroidery threads (matte cotton): red, orange, turquoise, yellow, steel blue, light green, dark green
- Blue thread
- Dark red thread
- 10cm (4in) turquoise zip
- 4cm (1½in) lobster swivel clip
- 18mm (¾in) silver 'D'-ring
- 18mm (¾in) silver magnetic clip
- 2 small silver rivets
- Scrap of turquoise ribbon
- Your usual sewing needs

Prepare the interfacings:

Using the templates, cut the interfacing – you will need two pieces of fusible interfacing (such as S320) for the flap (one for the lining and one for the outer), and one piece of fusible wadding/batting (such as H640) for the flap. For the main purse body you need two pieces of fusible interfacing (such as S320) and two pieces of fusible wadding/batting (such as H640). Cut two scraps of lightweight fusible interfacing (such as Decovil I Light) to reinforce the magnetic lock too.

The flap

1. Cut a piece of blue linen measuring 23 x 21cm (9 x 8¼in) and fuse it to the woven interfacing (such as G740; the woven interfacing will help to stop the linen from fraying without adding too much bulk). Cut a piece of lining fabric the same size as the linen and put it aside. Take the purse flap template and a water-soluble marker and draw around the flap shape onto the right side of the linen to help you position the embroidery.

2. Transfer the embroidery pattern onto the flap using your favourite method. Embroider the flowers and leaves using two strands of embroidery thread. Use straight stitch on the leaves (light green, dark green) and large flower (red, orange), chain stitch on the tulips (turquoise, steel blue) and lazy daisy stitch for the blossoms (steel blue). Finish with yellow French knot centres (a cluster for the large flower and one each for the little blossoms) – also add some random French knot fillers in orange. See pages 35–38 for embroidery stitch techniques.

3. When the embroidery is done, fuse the interfacing (such as S320) to the wrong side (this also keeps the thread ends secure by effectively gluing them into place between the interfacings). Then fuse the wadding/batting (such as H640) over the top of the interfacing – trust me, this works. The trick is to balance it so that it is in the right area and the embroidery is even. Hold it up to a window to help centre it.

4. On the lining piece, fuse the interfacing (such as S320) to the back, then reinforce the place where the magnetic clip will go (this is marked on the diagram) with a scrap of lightweight interfacing (such as Decovil I Light). Attach the male half of the magnetic clip set (see page 14).

5. Place the lining square and the wadded/interfaced linen piece right sides together and sew around the edge of the interfacing, right on the edge of the interfacing. Don't sew the top straight side. It is a bit fiddly to get the pieces all to line up, but you can feel your way with your fingers and then pin.

6. Cut the shape out with a 5mm (¹/₄in) seam allowance around the curved edges and a 1cm (³/₈in) seam allowance along the top straight edge. Clip into the curves and corners.

7. Turn the right way out, press and topstitch around the edge (I used blue top thread), again ignoring the top straight side. Trim evenly if need be so that the flap measures 12cm (4³/₄in) from the tip of the curve to the straight edge.

The front

8. Cut two pieces of red and white spotted linen, 21 x 16cm (8¹/₄ x 6¹/₂in), and fuse the interfacing (such as S320) on to the back of each. On the piece that will form the front of the bag, locate the place where the magnetic clip will go and reinforce this with a scrap of lightweight interfacing (such as Decovil I Light). Then add the wadding/batting (such as H640) to the back of each piece. Put the unreinforced piece (the back piece) to one side.

9. Cut a piece of woven ribbon 20cm (8in) long and topstitch it in place 3.5cm (1³/₈in) up from the bottom of the front side of the purse (it helps to roughly draw the purse shape on the right side of the linen with the water-soluble marker so that you can see where the ribbon goes – better than flying totally blind!).

10. Attach the other half of the magnetic clasp to the centre of the ribbon (see page 14).

11. Cut the purse shape out leaving a 5mm (¹/₄in) seam allowance all round.

The back

12. From the lining fabric, cut a piece for the pocket lining measuring 14cm wide by 24cm deep (5¹/₂ x 9¹/₂in).

13. On the back piece that you interfaced in step 8, mark a 10 x 1cm (4 x ³/₈in) zip box, 3.25cm (1¹/₄in) down from the top (see pages 22–23). Insert the zip and line the pocket with the lining pieces; the pocket lining sits flush with the top of the purse including the seam allowance.

14. Thread a piece of ribbon scrap through the zip pull.

15. Trim the purse back to shape, leaving a 5mm (¹/₄in) seam allowance. Attach the flap right sides together to the top centre edge of the trimmed back.

The lining

16. Use the trimmed front of the purse as a template to cut two pieces of lining.

17. Make a 7 x 10cm (2³/₄ x 4in) lined patch pocket for the back lining piece, and topstitch it in place 2.5cm (1in) from the top (see page 31).

Tab

18. Cut a piece of lining fabric 6 x 7cm (2¹/₂ x 2³/₄in). Fold it in half lengthways and crease. Fold the raw edges in and press. Topstitch along both sides.

19. Fold the tab in half and enclose the 'D'-ring. Secure with a silver rivet. Tack/baste to the left-hand side of the front of the purse, 2.5cm (1in) down from the top edge, as marked on the pattern; position right sides facing, aligning the raw edges.

Tip

This strap (unlike the other handles in the book) doesn't have any interfacing. That is because it is thin enough to be self-supporting. Any wider and it would be floppy without something to hold it up.

Strap

20. Cut a piece of lining fabric 6 x 31cm (2¹/₂ x 12in). Fold in half lengthways and press to crease. Fold the raw edges to the centre and press again. Open out and thread the swivel clip on. Sew the ends together to form a loop, then refold the creases and topstitch to close, moving the clip along as you sew. Keep the clip in place with a silver rivet (see page 32).

Putting it all together

21. Place the back lining piece (the one with the patch pocket) and lay it right sides together onto the back panel with the flap sandwiched in between. Sew along the top flat edge only.

22. Do the same on the front, aligning the front and lining piece right sides together. Open out the pieces (still ignoring the flap and the tab, save for keeping them where they should be) and pin lining to lining and outer to outer. Leaving a gap in the base of the lining, sew all around the edge.

23. Turn out through the gap and sew it closed.

24. Stuff the lining down into the purse and press very carefully to finish.

Liesl

This one is fresh from the high alpine pastures! It is a cute little bag for carrying the day's essentials and it even has some embroidery on the handle *sigh*. I have used my sewing machine to do this, but if yours doesn't do that sort of thing, simply buy some extra woven ribbon and topstitch it to the handle instead. Best of all, this little cutie is fat quarter-friendly!

Finished size: 23 x 23cm (9 x 9in), plus handle

The front

1. Use the template to cut the front piece of the bag from red and white floral fabric (A); transfer the dart marks from the template. Interface it with fusible wadding/batting (such as H640), then cut out the darts.

2. To create the circular motif, layer up the grey circle, the blue flower and then the alpine motif. Embroider the three layers together and into position on the centre front of the bag in one go. Use white thread to secure.

Tip

A dab of glue will help the motif pieces behave while you work.

3. Sew the darts, with right sides facing.

4. Cut a piece of grey and white spotted fabric (B) for the band using the template. Interface with fusible wadding/batting (such as H640). Attach the navy and white ruffle trim across the middle and then the woven ribbon over the top.

5. Sew the band to the top of the front piece, with right sides facing, then open out and press.

The back

6. Construct the back in exactly the same way as the front, but leave off the motif. Ensure that your ruffle trim is at the same height as on the front band, so that the trims will line up when you put the bag together.

The strap

7. Cut a strap from the grey and white spotted fabric (B) that measures 8cm (3$\frac{1}{8}$in) wide x 65cm (25 $\frac{2}{3}$in) long. Cut a piece of Bundfix tape 65cm (25 $\frac{2}{3}$in) long. Fuse the tape centrally to the wrong side of the fabric.

8. Make an open-ended strap (refer to page 33 if you need to): fold the raw edges in and then fold in half using the perforations as a guide. I finished the strap with a row of machine-stitched hearts in red thread (because it was just too cute not to) and this is a nice finishing touch. But it is by no means necessary – an extra 65cm (25 $\frac{2}{3}$in) of woven ribbon sewn to the centre of the strap will do just as nicely.

Gather these supplies

Fabrics
- A: 1 fat quarter red and white floral fabric, for the bag outer
- B: 35cm (14in) strip grey-and-white spotted fabric, for the strap and band
- C: 1 fat quarter coordinating fabric, for lining (I used the same grey-and-white spotted fabric as for the strap)

Interfacings
- 1 fat quarter fusible wadding/batting (such as H640)
- 1 fat eighth fusible interfacing (such as S320)
- 25cm (10in) strip lightweight fusible interfacing (such as Decovil I Light)
- Bundfix tape, 7cm (2¾in) wide

Everything else
- 50cm (20in) woven ribbon with an alpine theme
- 50cm (20in) navy and white gingham ruffle binding
- 7.5cm (3in) grey felt circle
- Large blue felt flower (template provided)
- Round alpine-inspired appliqué to fit the flower
- Glue
- Invisible magnetic clasp
- Coordinating threads for topstitching
- Water-soluble marker
- Your usual sewing needs

53

The lining

9. Cut two pieces of lining from your chosen fabric for the main part of the bag and two lining bands, using the templates.

10. Attach a 10 x 12cm (4 x 4³/₄in) lined patch pocket onto the right side of the back lining piece (see page 31). Use the fusible interfacing (such as S320) for this, along with some pretty outer fabric and lining. Attach with a narrow topstitch around the bottom and sides.

11. Cut two pieces of fusible interfacing (such as S320) for the lining bands using the template; attach the magnetic clasps in the very centre, see page 14, making sure that your magnets are facing the right way. Fuse the interfacing to the wrong side of the lining bands.

12. Sew the darts in the main lining pieces, and then join the bands on the top edges. Sew the two lining pieces together, right sides facing, around the outer edge – but leave a gap somewhere on the bottom for turning through later.

Putting it all together

13. With the right sides together, sew the front and the back pieces of the bag around the bottom and side edges.

14. Attach the straps to the top side edges of the bag; sew right sides together, aligning the raw edges, over the side seams.

15. With the lining inside out, pull it on over the top of the outer so that the right sides are together. Sew around the top. Turn the bag out through the gap, then hand stitch it closed. Topstitch around the top edge to finish.

Shirley

You cannot possibly have too many pretty totes – that is a rule I live by. This one could be made from any fabric and used at any time of the year, but make it in the softest of spring colours and it is just asking to be taken out at Easter time. I love the idea of bags for different seasons – imagine the same one made in a knobbly tweed for autumn.

Finished size: 55 x 40 x 10cm (21²/₃ x 15¾ x 4in), plus handles

The handles

1. Cut a piece of Bundfix tape 140cm (55¹/₄in) long. Cut a piece of fabric C the same length as the tape but 10cm (4in) wide. Fuse the tape to the wrong side of the fabric, allowing some fabric overhang each side.

2. Fold the raw edges in and fold the tape in half to make a strap 3.5cm (1¹/₂in) wide. Topstitch twice down each side with coordinating thread and then cut the strap in half to make two handles (see page 33).

Tip

When you have a striped fabric, I find that it works better to cut across the pattern rather than having one or two stripes running down.

The front

3. Cut the following:

The front panel cutting list

From fabric B, cut a bottom strip 60 x 15cm (23²/₃ x 6in)

From fabric A, cut two front panels 34.5 x 20cm (13½ x 8in) each

From fabric B, cut a middle panel 24 x 34.5cm (9½ x 13½in)

From fabric E and from lining, cut a pocket measuring 24cm (9½in) square

4. Make the pocket by cutting a piece of wadding/batting 25cm (10in) square. Place the pocket fabric over the top of it and channel quilt with vertical lines about 1cm (³/₈in) apart. We are quilting vertically here so that in the next step the topstitching will not compete with the rows of quilting.

5. Trim the wadding/batting back to the size of the pocket front and lay the lining right sides together over the pocket. Sew along the top edge only and then fold the lining over and press. Topstitch the top edge narrowly.

6. Align all the layers and then tack/baste the sides and bottom of the pocket. Don't worry about neatening the raw edges, as these will be taken up in the seams.

Gather these supplies

Fabrics
- A: 50cm (½yd) pink floral, for front side panels and bag back
- B: 30cm (12in) grey, for base and front centre panel
- C: 30cm (12in) pink patterned, for handles and patch pockets
- D: 1m (1yd) mint floral, for lining
- E: 30cm (12in) mint patterned, for front pocket

Interfacings
- 1.5m (60in) sew-in foam interfacing (such as Style-Vil)
- 1m (39½in) 80/20 cotton mix wadding/batting (such as #279)
- 1 fat quarter fusible interfacing (such as S320)
- Bundfix tape, 7cm (2¾in) wide

Everything else
- Coordinating threads for topstitching
- 18cm (7in) aqua zip
- 2 grey plastic snap fasteners
- Ribbon scrap for the zip pull
- Extra bits and pieces for the embellishment: wool, cotton yarn, beads, small swivel clip, perle coton, 'D'-ring
- Your usual sewing needs

57

Here is the list of Art Gallery Fabrics I used, in case you want to use the same:

- A: Yinghua Cherrylight
- B: Cool Foliage smooth solid denim
- C: Zhu Nectar
- D: Yinghua Rainwater
- E: Zhu Mist

7. Take the fabric C middle panel and cut a piece of wadding/batting slightly larger. Lay the fabric over the wadding/batting and channel quilt it on the diagonal; space the lines about 1cm ($^3/_8$in) apart. Trim the wadding/batting back and lay the pocket over the quilted panel. Pin and tack/baste the edges together.

8. Install a plastic snap fastener to connect the top centre edge of the central pocket and the middle panel.

9. The two side panels and the bottom panel come next. As in step 7, layer the fabric pieces onto pieces of wadding/batting slightly larger and then quilt (horizontally this time), before trimming to size.

10. Sew the two side panels to the middle pocket section, and then sew the bottom panel to the bottom. Press and trim all around.

11. To get the basic bag shape, we do not need a template. Mark the vertical centre on the top edge. From this mark, measure 30cm (12in) either side and make a mark at the same level.

12. Do the same on the bottom edge: find the bottom centre mark, but this time measure 25cm (10in) either side of it and make a mark.

13. Draw a straight line across the top and across the bottom, accurately stopping at the marks. Join the bottom left and top left, and bottom right and top right points to make a sort of inverted trapezoid. Cut the shape out. This is the front of the bag.

14. Lay the bag front onto a piece of slightly larger foam interfacing and sew around the outside with a narrow seam. Trim back the foam interfacing.

Tip

The idea of this bag is that it gets a feeling of movement from the different directions of quilting, so choose a slightly different direction for each panel and always choose a coordinating thread where possible.

The back

15. The bottom section of the back is the same as on the front: cut a piece from fabric B measuring 60 x 15cm (23²/₃ x 6in). Back it with wadding/batting, channel quilt it and then trim it. The rest of the back is made from fabric A and it measures 60 x 34.5cm (23²/₃ x 13¹/₂in). Back with wadding/batting and then quilt this with horizontal lines, as you did for the front side panels.

16. Cut a piece of pocket lining measuring 25cm wide by 50cm long (10 x 20in).

17. At the centre of the back panel, measure down 5cm (2in) from the top and mark a 1 x 18cm (³/₈ x 7in) zip box. Install the zip, then sew the sides and bottom of the lining to complete the pocket. Finish with a piece of ribbon through the zip pull (see pages 22–23).

18. Sew the bottom piece onto the main piece and then press. Using the front piece as a template, trim the back panel into the same inverted trapezoid shape.

19. Lay the back panel onto a piece of foam interfacing and attach with a narrow seam. Trim the foam interfacing back.

The lining

20. Use the front of the bag as a template to cut two pieces of lining fabric.

21. Make two patch pockets measuring 25 x 15cm (10 x 6in). Use fabric C for the pocket outers and line with fusible interfacing (such as S320) and fabric D (see page 31).

22. Attach the pockets to the lining pieces – one on the front and one on the back – with a narrow topstitch seam and divide them with a vertical seam or seams as required.

23. Lay the front and back lining pieces together and sew the sides and bottom, but leave a large turning gap in the bottom edge. Draw a 5cm (2in) square in each corner and then cut it out. Pinch off the corners and box the bottom (see page 25).

Putting it all together

24. Lay the front and back outer pieces together, right sides facing, and sew the sides and bottom without gaps. Draw a 5cm (2in) square in each corner and then cut it out. Pinch the corners off and box the bottom (see page 25).

25. With a narrow seam, attach the straps to the front and back, right sides facing, 14.5cm (5³/₄in) in from each edge.

26. With the outer the right way out and the lining inside out, pull the lining on over the outer and then sew around the top leaving no gaps. Turn the bag out through the gap in the lining and then sew the gap closed.

27. Stuff the lining down into the bag and topstitch around the top edge. Attach another plastic snap fastener to the top edge in the middle to keep the bag closed.

The embellishment

28. This bag will be roomy enough for all of your needs but it can look a bit sparse if left unadorned. A simple clip-on embellishment, made from a pompom and a tassel with some beads, does the trick. Make a large pompom from grey wool and smaller pompoms from pink, blue and green yarn (look up instructions online if you're not sure how – it's very simple!)

29. Make a tassel from the pink cotton yarn and leave a nice long tail of perle coton at the top. Thread the beads on and then thread the whole lot through the pompom. Attach a swivel clip at the top and then pass the thread back through the beads a couple of times to make it strong.

30. Attach the large 'D'-ring to the handle and clip on the charm. I have added a ribbon scrap as well because it looked a bit bare at the top without it. See what you like yourself and use what you have.

Tilde

You have to love a handy tote – perfect for shopping or even as storage in your home. Imagine a few of these bags hanging in the hallway instead of a pile of winter hats and scarves.

Finished size: 37 x 35 x 10cm (14½ x 13¾ x 4in), plus strap

The front

1. Begin by cutting strips from five of your fat eighths that each measure 9 x 27cm (3½ x 10¾in). Sew them together to form a panel 40 x 26cm (15¾ x 10¼in).

> ### Tip
> Use any fabrics that take your fancy to get a colourful, scrappy result.

2. Use the template to cut a top section from another fabric (I used patterned blue). Sew this to the strip panel and press.

3. Make a straight grain binding trim from your solid navy fabric (see page 28). You will need about 80cm (31½in) total; 40cm (15¾in) for the front and back.

4. Cut a piece of lightweight fusible interfacing that measures 10 x 15cm (4 x 6in) and fuse it to the wrong side of the bag top, directly where the handle cut-out will be. Round off the corners to eliminate any sharp bits, which can work their way through the fabric with time and wear.

5. Sew the whole front piece to a piece of foam interfacing using a half normal seam allowance around the outside edge; trim back.

6. Quilt alongside each of the sewn seams and attach the straight binding to the join between the strip panel and the top. Swap to the coordinating thread for this bit.

7. Cut out the handle: use the template to position it exactly and then draw it with a water-soluble marker – it is helpful to make a template from card and just trace around it onto the fabric.

8. Sew around the handle on the line that you just drew. It is handy to sew around the handle gap like this because you can then see if it is in the dead centre (and it has to be). If it isn't, it is not too late to unpick and go again. Cut inside the line, leaving about 5mm (¼in) seam allowance.

The back

9. Make this in exactly the same way as the front, but consider using different strips for the bottom section; personally, I think the top back looks better if it is made from the same fabric as the top front.

Gather these supplies

Fabrics
- Fat eighths of 8 different fabrics
- 75cm (30in) pink script, for linings
- 25cm (10in) patterned blue, for the bag top, front and back
- 1 fat quarter navy, for binding

Interfacings
- 1m (39½in) foam interfacing (such as Style-Vil)
- Bundfix tape, 7cm (2¾in) wide
- 25 x 25cm (10 x 10in) lightweight fusible interfacing (such as Decovil I Light)

Everything else
- 2 18cm (7in) navy zips
- 2 2.5cm (1in) silver 'D'-rings
- 2 2.5cm (1in) silver swivel clips
- 1 2.5cm (1in) silver bag slider
- 1 blue plastic snap fastener
- Thread to coordinate with your solid
- Bottom reinforcing mesh
- Water-soluble marker
- Your usual sewing needs

Here is the list of Art Gallery Fabrics I used, in case you want to use the same:

- Fat eighths: Bedside Journal Sunny, Lotus Beats Echo, Block Festival, Where the Heart is Pure, Table Flowers Rainbow, Entryways Candied, Forget Me Not Calm, Window View Spring
- Lining: To Live by Love
- Bag top: Grass in Moonlight

The lining

10. Use the template to cut two whole pieces from the lining fabric. Iron a vertical centre crease in both.

11. On each piece, measure down 20cm (8in) from the top centre on the wrong side of the fabric and draw a zip box 18 x 1cm (7 x $^3/_8$in) centrally, using the folds to guide you.

12. Also from the lining fabric, cut two pieces 26cm wide by 32cm long ($10^1/_4$ x $12^1/_2$in). These will form the zip box linings. Insert the box style zips using one lining piece per pocket. Bring the long end up and sew the sides and top (see pages 22–23). Normally, the pocket lining sits flush with the top of the main bag lining, but this time it cannot do that because of the handle cut-out. Instead, simply bring the end of the lining up so that it is above the zip and even with the other part. Sometimes, if there is not very much room, a zip foot will do the job better for you.

The strap

13. Cut strips of fabric measuring 7cm ($2^3/_4$in) wide – you are aiming for about 185cm (73in) length in total, so join them together if you have to. Fuse to the Bundfix, fold in and topstitch along the length on both sides (see page 33).

14. Cut 20cm (8in) off one end for the tabs. Secure the end to the centre bar of the slider. Take the other end through a swivel clip, back through the bag slider and then to the other swivel clip where you can secure it by hand or machine.

The tabs

15. Make the tabs by cutting the tab section in half to make two pieces 10cm (4in) long. Fold them in half and insert a 'D'-ring in each. (You will sew a tab into the side seam, 2.5cm (1in) down from the top on each side when you sew the bag up, in step 19.)

Putting it all together

16. Place a lining piece right sides together with an outer and pin. Sew around the handle hole and cut the handle out of the lining. Snip carefully around the edge of the handle hole and post the lining through the hole, just as you did for the zip.

17. Smooth the lining down on the back of the outer panel and topstitch around the handle hole. Repeat for the other outer and lining pieces.

18. Place the lining pieces right sides together and sew around the two sides and bottom only. Box the corners by cutting a 4cm (1¹/₂in) square (see page 25).

Tip

Step 18 is a fiddly operation and it is better if you can pin the bit that you are not working on up out of the way, as you did when you lined the pockets.

19. Sew the outside pieces together, right sides facing; tuck a tab in each side with a 'D'-ring enclosed, about 2.5cm (1in) from the top edge. Box the corners to match the lining.

20. You will see a gap by the handle hole – turn the bag out through that and check to see that everything is sitting nicely.

21. Cut a piece of mesh to fit the base and trim as needed. Hot glue it in place and glue a bit of spare wadding/batting over the top to pad it a bit.

22. Make about 102cm (40in) of bias binding from your navy solid (see page 27).

23. Tack/baste the lining to the top curve of the bag and bind that edge with bias binding.

24. Install a plastic snap fastener to connect the outer pieces, underneath the handle hole.

Hannah

The bright colours here are really eye-catching. I love this combination of turquoise and green together and I tend to use it a lot. The different textures on the stitched front panel make this special too. But don't worry if you are new to embroidery; it is all very easy, and only one or two stitches are used to get this folksy look.

Finished size: 19.5cm across x 6.5cm deep (7¾ x 2½in), plus strap

The front

1. From the green and white gingham (fabric A), cut a square that measures 24cm (9½in). Cut a piece of wadding/batting the same size, and fuse this to the back of the fabric. Use the template to draw a circle in the middle of it.

2. Using the template, cut a large turquoise felt flower, five green hearts, a smaller white flower and a green circle. Arrange the motif as you see in the diagram and glue the pieces into place on the marked circle.

3. Using long straight hand stitches, embroider the details as you see on the template (see page 35). The blue threads are worked on the white flower and the hearts and the white threads on the large turquoise blossom. Finish with free-motion embroidery to secure the felt motifs to the gingham.

4. Trim the circle and lay on top of a slightly larger piece of foam interfacing. Attach with a half normal seam and then trim the layers even.

Gather these supplies

Fabrics
- A: 1 fat quarter of green and white gingham fabric, for bag front and gusset
- B: 1 fat quarter of rich turquoise floral fabric, for strap and binding
- C: 30cm (12in) strip light turquoise fabric, for zip panel and patch pockets
- D: 1 fat quarter of solid turquoise fabric, for lining

Interfacings
- 1 fat quarter of dense quilt wadding/batting (such as Thermolam)
- 1 fat quarter of foam interfacing (such as Style-Vil)
- 1 fat quarter of fusible interfacing (such as S320)
- Bundfix tape, 7cm (2¾in) wide

Everything else
- Squares of green, white and turquoise felt
- Coordinating thread for topstitching
- Perle 8 coton in rich blue and white
- 2 18cm (7in) zips
- Coordinating beads
- Glue
- Strong thread for beading
- 2 2.5cm (1in) silver rectangle rings
- Your usual sewing needs

The back

5. Use the template to cut a 21cm (8¼in) circle from rich turquoise fabric (B). Cut a rectangle of light turquoise floral for pocket lining, measuring 18 x 32cm (7 x 12½in).

6. Make a box zip 6cm (2½in) down from the top of the fabric circle (see pages 22–23). The box zip should be 1 x 11cm (³⁄₈ x 4½in) long, so you will have to trim the zip back. Use a central crease to get it perfectly positioned.

7. Fold the pocket lining up and sew the sides and top to complete the pocket. You may need to trim the pocket a bit to make it fit perfectly. It is slightly generous for this reason. Fit and then adjust – you can always trim fabric away!

8. Lay the whole back piece onto a piece of foam interfacing and attach with a narrow seam. Trim the interfacing back.

The gusset

9. Prepare the end of the zip that opens by stitching it together to secure the ends.

10. Cut two fabric tabs, 5.5 x 5.5cm (2¼ x 2¼in). Fold one side of each tab over by 1cm (³⁄₈in) and topstitch a tab to each end of the zip.

11. For the sides of the zip, cut two turquoise floral pieces (C) 4cm wide x 24.5cm long (1½ x 9¾in). Cut two pieces of lining the same. Attach the outer pieces to foam interfacing and trim.

12. With the right sides together, add a floral strip to each side of the zip and then turn over and topstitch. Repeat for the other side and then trim the end tabs – they will now be mostly concealed; see image opposite, top right. The zip section should now measure 24.5 x 7cm (9¾ x 2¾in).

13. Take a piece of lining and fold one long edge over by 5mm (¼in) and press. Hand sew (I know, I know – but sometimes it is necessary) to the wrong side of the zip to hide all of the goings on. Repeat for the other side.

14. Stitch the long side edges of the lining to the interfaced top of the zip sides to give it some structure and trim away any excess.

15. You will notice that there are a couple of areas which are quite unattractive at each end of the zip on the inside. Cut a piece of lining slightly larger than the area and topstitch it over the top, hiding the problem; do this by hand with a coordinating thread. The raw edges will be taken care of in the side binding.

16. The rest of the 'gusset' section comprises a piece of green gingham outer fabric, 40 x 7.5cm (15¾ x 3in), a piece of lining the same size and a piece of foam interfacing slightly larger.

17. Use a half normal seam to attach the outer fabric to the foam interfacing and then flip it over and attach the lining the same way. Trim the foam interfacing back.

18. Sew the gusset into one 'tube', by sewing the green gingham strip to the ends of the zipped panel with right sides facing.

The lining

19. Cut two 21cm (8¼in) circles of lining. Make a couple of 12 x 10cm (4¾ x 4in) lined patch pockets to fit inside (see page 31). Use the fusible interfacing (such as S320) for this and remember to cut the interfacing to the size that you want the pocket to be and then make the outer fabric and lining slightly larger. You then trim the fabric and lining back when the pocket is finished. One of my pockets is a double one. If you like this, simply make two pockets and put one over the other. There are a couple of things to remember though: obviously, one is lower than the other so that you can see the one behind, but what isn't so obvious is to cut the front one a tiny amount larger than the back one so that the two seams on top of each other are not too bulky (see page 31 for adding pockets).

> *Tip*
>
> Mark which way is up so that when you put the lining in, everything is aligned properly – this is not always obvious on a circle!

20. The linings will be stitched to the back of the interfaced outer circles. This will be put together in one go and then the raw edges are hidden in the binding.

The strap and tabs

21. Cut a piece of Bundfix tape 110cm (43^1/$_2$in) long and fuse it to the centre back of a piece of rich turquoise fabric the same length but 10cm (4in) wide.

22. Fold the edges in and topstitch down both sides (using coordinating thread) to make a 2.5cm (1in) wide strap. Trim the ends.

23. Cut 20cm (8in) off the end and then cut that in half to make two 10cm (4in) tabs to carry the rectangle rings.

24. Fold the tabs over, enclosing a ring in each. Topstitch to the zip panel bottom (on the green and white gingham fabric) 2.5cm (1in) down from the side seam.

Tip

These tabs have raw ends, which you don't want to see on the final product. To get rid of this problem, don't put the rectangle ring in the centre of the tab. Instead, form the tab into a loop with the raw edges hidden and overlapping by about 1cm (^{3}/$_8$in) – these ends should sit against the fabric and be hidden.

Putting it all together

25. Take the front circle and the lining piece destined for that side. Decide which way is up and then pin the lining onto the back of the front panel, wrong sides facing. Stitch around to hold them together – use zigzag stitch; it is a great way to do this and make the edge really flat for binding.

26. Do the same on the back panel and second lining piece.

27. You will need to make about 140cm (55in) of bias binding, using the rich turquoise fabric (see page 27).

28. Apply the first edge of the bias binding to the front and back pieces too at this point (see steps 1–2, page 28). It is far less fiddly to do it now than it would be when the side panel is there too. This way it only needs to be hand finished when everything is sewn together. I like to machine sew the binding to the front side and then hand finish it on the back.

29. Sew the front piece to the zipped side section, then repeat for the back piece.

30. Finish off the binding by hand.

31. Attach the strap by posting it through the rings and stitching in place to secure.

32. Make some little beaded charms and stitch them to the zip pulls (see page 43).

Claudia

I love the way that the rougher linen keeps these lovely prints from being too sweet; it grounds the whole project. What you have is a pretty bag, perfect for use when the days are bright – or else in the winter when everything is grey and your soul needs a pop of colour.

Finished size: 33 x 23 x 10cm (13 x 9 x 4in), plus strap

The back

1. Cut a piece of denim (A) measuring 36 x 22cm (14$^1/_4$ x 8$^3/_4$in). Cut a piece of fabric B to 36 x 10cm (14$^1/_4$ x 4in). Sew the floral to the denim and press.

2. Cut a piece of lining fabric (B) to 25cm wide by 50cm long (10 x 20in) – this is for the zip pocket lining. Make a vertical crease to find the centre.

3. Make a vertical crease to find the centre of the floral/denim panel. Measure down 3.5cm (1$^3/_8$in) from the top edge and make a mark on the wrong side of the floral panel. Site an 18 x 1cm (7 x $^3/_8$in) zip box on this mark in the centre of the panel. Install the zip (see pages 22–23).

4. Complete the zip pocket by folding up the lining and sewing the sides and top – use the vertical crease marks to help you centre it.

5. Sew the completed bag back onto a piece of foam interfacing that measures 32 x 36cm (12$^1/_2$ x 14$^1/_4$in), with a narrow seam, and trim neatly.

Gather these supplies

Fabrics
- A: 40cm (15$^3/_4$in) blue denim-linen for bag front and back lower panels
- B: 40cm (15$^3/_4$in) pink check, for lining
- C: 1 fat eighth green check, for pockets
- D: 1 fat eighth floral, for top band
- E: 25cm (10in) mint floral, for strap and button tab

Interfacings
- 35cm (14in) strip foam interfacing (such as Style-Vil)
- 1 fat eighth fusible wadding/batting (such as H630)
- 1 fat quarter fusible interfacing (such as S320)
- Bundfix tape, 7cm (2$^3/_4$in) wide

Everything else
- 18cm (7in) mint zip
- 2 40mm (1$^1/_2$in) silver square rings
- 1 40mm (1$^1/_2$in) silver bag slider
- Large coordinating button
- Sew-in magnetic clasp
- Plastic snap fastener to match the button
- Coordinating threads for topstitching
- Base mesh
- Your usual sewing needs

71

Here is the list of Art Gallery Fabrics I used, in case you want to use the same:
- B: Seeds of Dahlia
- C: Trellis Plaid Fresh
- D: Mother's Garden Rich
- E: Sun Print Fern

The front

6. Make a tab from fabric E: cut two pieces 6 x 11cm ($2^1/_2$ x $4^3/_8$in) and fuse one to a piece of fusible wadding/batting. Attach one half of the magnetic snap to the bottom of the interfaced piece (see page 14).

7. Sew the two tab pieces right sides together around the bottom edge and the two long sides, then turn through and topstitch around the outside. Sew on the button.

8. Cut a piece of fabric A measuring 36 x 22cm ($14^1/_4$ x $8^3/_4$in). Cut a piece of fabric B to 10 x 36cm (4 x $14^1/_4$in). Crease the denim vertically to find the centre and press.

9. Tack/baste the tab on the centre crease with a narrow seam. Sew the floral to the denim fabric, right sides facing, then open out and press.

10. You will need to decorate the front of the patch pocket with the denim strip and label before you line it. Cut fabric C for the pocket to 17 x 12cm ($6^2/_3$ x $4^3/_4$in).

11. Create an 18cm (7in) length of flat binding from the denim fabric (see page 28). Sew this to the pocket, 4cm ($1^1/_2$in) up from the bottom. Tuck a cute label under the denim strip as you sew it on. Don't forget to use your double-sided tape to keep things straight without pins!

12. Interface the pocket front with fusible wadding/batting, and then line it (see page 31). Turn it through and then sew in the other half of the magnetic snap in the centre, 3cm ($1^1/_4$in) down from the front edge.

13. Sew the front of the bag to a piece of foam interfacing slightly larger all around with a narrow seam, and trim. Topstitch either side of the denim/floral seam.

The strap

14. Cut a strip of fabric E 10cm wide and 120cm long (4 x $47^1/_2$in) – join pieces of fabric to make up the length if you need to. Cut a strip of Bundfix tape 120cm ($47^1/_2$in) long. Fuse the tape to the centre of the wrong side of the fabric.

15. Fold the raw edges in and then fold in half using the perforations as a guide. Topstitch five times along the length of the strap at equal intervals (see page 33). Join it to the middle bar of the bag slider. The strap will be put on last as it can get in the way otherwise.

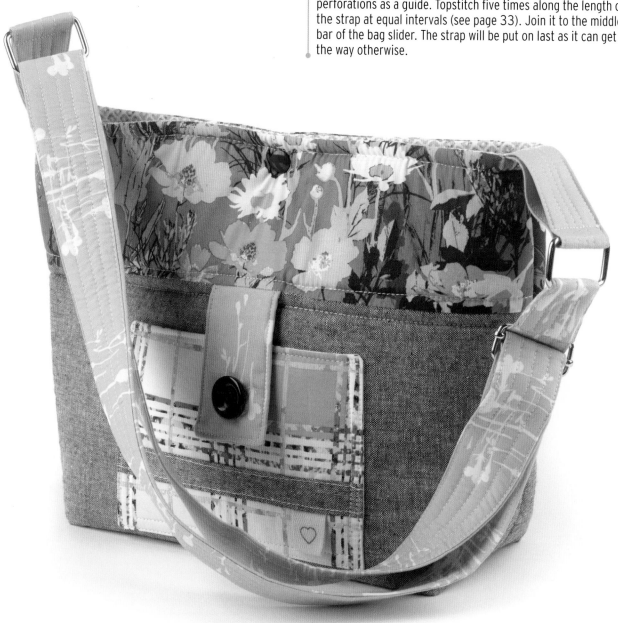

The tabs

16. Make two tabs 15cm long and 4cm wide (6 x 1¹/₂in); for this you will need two strips of fabric E, 15 x 10cm (6 x 4in) and a 30cm (12in) length of Bundfix tape. Fuse the Bundfix to the centre of each fabric tab, fold the raw edges in and then fold in half using the perforations as a guide (see page 33). Topstitch five times along the length of each at equal intervals.

The lining

17. Cut two pieces of fabric B, 32 x 36cm (12¹/₂ x 14¹/₄in).

18. Add a lined patch pocket to each lining piece using fabric C, your lining fabric and pieces of fusible interfacing (see page 31). My pockets measure 15 x 22cm (6 x 8²/₃in), but choose the size that you need. Just make sure that they are not too big or they will get caught up in the sides when you box the corners. If you need to, use vertical seams to create compartments and stop the pockets from sagging.

19. With right sides facing, sew the sides and base of the two lining pieces together, leaving a 15cm (6in) gap in one side. Cut out a 5cm (2in) square from the two bottom corners. Box the corners (see page 25).

Putting it all together

20. Place the outer bag pieces together, with right sides facing, and sew the sides and base. Cut out a 5cm (2in) square from the two bottom corners. Box the corners (see page 25).

21. Cut a piece of mesh 23 x 9cm (9 x 3¹/₂in) and hot glue it into the base of the bag.

22. Attach the tabs to each end of the bag, right sides facing, aligning the raw edges, with a square ring in place on each.

23. Turn the lining inside out. Slip the outer bag (which is the right way out) inside, so that the right sides of the outer and lining fabrics are touching. Sew right the way around the top of the bag, then turn the bag out the right way through the gap in the lining.

24. Topstitch around the top edge of the bag, then attach the shoulder strap.

25. Add the plastic snap fastener to the centre top edge of the bag.

Lotte

This design has bags of very on-trend Alpine chic! It is easy to make and very practical. It holds a lot, too, and you can find things in a second. This bag is even easier because it has no zips, making it a great choice if you are a little new at this. It's an über-stylish bag with a professional finish.

Finished size: 50 x 40 x 10cm (20 x 15¾ x 4in)

The front

You will notice some lines on the template: it is very important that when you cut out the various parts that the LOWEST line is the cutting line for the top part of the bag and the UPPERMOST line is the cutting line for the bottom of the bag. This gives you your seam allowances automatically.

1. From the grey fabric (A), cut a bag upper part; from the felt (B), cut a lower piece. Sew them together and press.

2. Fuse a larger piece of wadding/batting onto the back of the bag panel – trim the wadding/batting so that it is about 2cm (around 1in) larger than the bag.

3. Use the water-soluble marker and the template to trace the handle opening and then cut it out.

> ### Tip
> The seam allowances in this bag have already been added but you may still have to trim the handle opening when it is sewn.

4. Quilt the grey top part of the bag in a classic grid pattern of diagonal squares, 2.5cm (1in) apart. I did this by hand for effect, but machine sewing is just as nice. Trim back the excess wadding/batting.

5. Lay the bag front onto a piece of slightly larger foam interfacing and pin – don't sew it just yet though. There is a bit of topstitching and embroidering to come and pinning helps to keep the layers together. Take the wide woven braid and attach it 15cm (6in) up from the bottom of the bag. Sew on the top edge only at this stage. Lining this up will be important when we sew the bag together – it is vital to match the side seams very accurately.

6. Tuck the red and white gingham ruffle under the bottom edge of the braid and sew it in place. Use a thread to match your braid.

> ### Tip
> Double-sided tape can be much better than pins for keeping things straight and in position as you sew.

Gather these supplies

Fabrics
- A: 1m (1yd) grey patterned fabric, for upper bag outer and binding
- B: 30cm (12in) dark grey marle pure wool felt, for bag base
- C: 60cm (23⅔in) strip red checked or tartan fabric, for lining
- 1 fat eighth of red polka dot fabric, for patch pocket
- Scrap of red and white gingham
- Scrap of black fabric

Interfacings
- 70cm (27⅗in) fusible wadding/batting (such as H630)
- 1m (39½in) foam interfacing (such as Style-Vil)

Everything else
- Small square of green felt
- 1m (39½in) wide woven braid (if you cannot find a wide braid that you like, consider making some with a beautiful fabric: cut a strip 8cm/3¼in wide and as long as needed on the straight of the grain, fold the edges under, sort of like bias binding, then topstitch to attach as you would braid)
- 1m (39½in) gathered red and white gingham ruffle trim (this is elastic)
- 1 red grosgrain bow
- 122cm (48in) red bias binding, bought or homemade (see page 27)
- Red perle 5 cotton
- Black sewing thread
- Fabric glue
- Pinking shears
- Water-soluble marker
- Label-making things (optional) – you will need a stamp of your choice, red ink, and a piece of cotton tape long enough to fold in half and stamp and still have a 5mm (¼in) seam allowance
- Your usual sewing needs

The label

7. This bag features a tab label (see pages 44–45), which will be attached on the right-hand side about 6cm (2$\frac{1}{2}$in) down from the top in the side seam. I used red ink, and my stamp is a cross stitch heart from a Christmas set – of all places! – which suits the vibe beautifully. It goes to prove that you should look at your craft stash from many different angles!

The patch

8. Cut an 11cm (4$\frac{1}{2}$in) circle from the green felt and pink the edge. Cut a slightly smaller circle from the red gingham scrap and glue it to the felt. Glue might seem a funny thing to use in a sewing pattern, but it is the business! It will keep the fabric layers from migrating. Trust me, fabric moves and you cannot stop it. Glue really helps.

Tip

Opt for muted tones to match this hunting lodge style of bag. If you choose a really bright green for the felt, for example, it just won't look right. Don't worry about it looking drab though – the job of the red and white gingham is to jolly it up, and it does this beautifully.

9. Next, using the template, cut the deer's head only from the black fabric, and glue it to the bottom of the patch.

10. Set your machine up for free-motion embroidery (FME). Draw the antlers onto the patch with the water-soluble marker and then sew them in black thread. Snip the stray threads close to the fabric.

11. Position the patch in the middle of the woven ribbon on the front. Complete the FME by going around the edge of the gingham about three times with black thread. Carefully clip the threads away very close to the appliqué. They won't fray out because the stitch is very tight.

12. Attach the bow to the bottom.

13. Swap back to normal sewing and attach the front panel around the edges to the foam interfacing – don't forget to sew around the handle opening very narrowly too to keep the interfacing and the outer together. Trim the foam back when you are done and cut the handle hole.

The back

14. Make exactly the same as for the front but omit the deer head motif. Remember to very carefully match the braid and ribbon on the front and back.

The lining

15. The lining is made using the same pattern template. Cut two pieces and mark and cut the handle holes.

16. I added an unlined patch pocket to the back piece of lining, measuring 15 x 23cm (6 x 9in). Simply cut your fabric to 16 x 24cm (6$\frac{1}{2}$ x 9$\frac{1}{2}$in), press under a narrow double hem and then topstitch in place about 2in (5cm) below the handle hole. Sew pocket divisions to suit your needs.

17. Place the back lining piece face down onto the back outer panel and line up the handle holes.

18. Pin well and sew around the handle hole. Clip the curve around the handle hole and then pull the fabric through the hole and smooth it down. Iron it well and then topstitch around the handle hole with the red perle cotton. Use a neat hand running stitch, or sew on your machine. Also make a row of red running stitch just above the woven ribbon, but tuck the lining out of the way when you do it. Repeat for the front lining and outer pieces.

Putting it all together

It is very important to sew the sides and base only and leave the top completely open. Because of the bag design, the best way to complete the top is with bias binding. We will look at that in the final steps.

19. Sew up the outer sides and base and then sew up the lining sides and base, right sides together. You will need to pull things up and out of the way to do this. Take advantage of the open top to manoeuvre things around. It actually feels and looks like a bit of a muddle but it does work out in the end.

20. Cut a square out of the lining and outer bottom corners, 2cm (³/₄in) in from the seams; box the corners (see page 25).

> ### Tip
>
> There is no need to leave a gap in the lining of this bag. There will be enough gap in the top just next to the handle on either side to turn the bag out.

21. Turn the bag out the right way through the gap in the side top. Stabilise the top edge with a running stitch made by hand – you won't see this when you are finished. Trim all layers the same, keeping the graceful curve of the bag.

22. Attach the red bias binding trim all the way around and keep the seam very narrow.

23. Using your grey patterned fabric A, make 122cm (48in) of bias binding (see page 27).

24. Bind the top edge again with your homemade bias binding as you would normally (see page 28). The red trim will peek out from under it.

Minna

If you are looking for a simple design to begin your bag making journey, you may have found it here! This backpack looks complicated but it is a zip-free zone and the techniques are fairly repetitive. Definitely one for boosting the ego!

Finished size: 31 x 39 x 9cm (12¼ x 15½ x 3½in), plus straps

The front

1. Cut a piece of fabric A, 21.5 x 41cm (8½ x 16in). This will form the top part of the front. Cut a second coordinating piece of fabric B, 23 x 41cm (9 x 16in) for the bottom of the front. Sew them together and press.

2. Sew the whole piece to a piece of slightly larger piece of foam interfacing using a half-normal seam. Trim the foam interfacing back to size.

3. Using the brown linen (E), cut a 3.5 x 41cm (1⅜ x 16in) strip. Fold, then press the long raw edges under so that the strip measures 15mm (⅔in) wide. Topstitch the strip in place over the join in the fabrics, along both long edges, using coordinating thread.

The front pocket

4. Cut a piece of fusible interfacing (such as S320), 17.5 x 16.5cm (7 x 6½in). Cut a piece of green floral fabric and a piece of lining fabric to 20 x 20cm (8 x 8in). Centre the interfacing shape onto the back of the outer fabric and fuse.

5. Cut a small piece of lightweight interfacing (such as Decovil I Light) to reinforce where the magnetic clasp will go – I sited mine about 7.5cm (3in) down from the top of the interfacing that is already attached. Fuse this on the back, over the attached interfacing, in the middle.

6. Install the female half of the magnetic clasp (see page 14).

7. With the right asides together (lining and fused outer), sew around the interfacing edge leaving a gap in the bottom. Trim the seam allowance back to 5mm (¼in). Turn out through the gap and press neatly.

8. Measure down 18cm (7in) from the top of the front bag panel and site the pocket. Topstitch into place along the sides and bottom edge (see also page 31).

Gather these supplies

Fabrics
- A: 1 fat quarter mint floral, for the upper front and back panels
- B: 1 fat quarter coordinating pattern, for the lower front and back panels
- C: 30cm (12in) coordinating pattern, for straps
- D: 1m (39½in) coordinating pattern, for lining
- E: 1 fat quarter brown linen
- 20cm (8in) square green floral, for the outer pocket
- 30cm (12.5in) coordinating pattern, for the inner patch pockets
- 8 x 41cm (3¼ x 16in) red check, for the back bottom strip

Interfacings
- 1m (39½in) foam interfacing (such as Style-Vil)
- 1 fat quarter fusible interfacing (such as S320)
- 1 fat quarter of lightweight fusible interfacing (such as Decovil I Light)
- 30cm (12in) fusible wadding/batting (such as H630)

Everything else
- 2 silver magnetic clasps
- 2 pretty crochet flowers, different but picking out a colour from the fabric
- 2 cute buttons
- Coordinating threads for topstitching
- 2 4cm (1½in) silver rectangle rings
- 2 4cm (1½in) silver bag sliders
- 30 x 9cm (12 x 3½in) foam board
- 2 coordinating plastic snap fasteners
- Your usual sewing needs

Here is the list of Art Gallery Fabrics I used, in case you want to use the same:

- A: Sprayed Blooms Bright
- B: Evenly Smudged Joy
- C: Angular Strings Coated
- D: Aerosol Stipple Smooth
- Outer pocket: Let's Chalk Green
- Patch pockets: Writings on Walls
- Back strip: Short Lines Burst

The pocket flap

9. Cut a rectangle of linen and a rectangle of lining fabric measuring 22 x 14cm (8³/₄ x 5¹/₂in). Using the pocket flap template, cut two shapes from fusible interfacing (such as S320). Fuse one interfacing shape to the wrong side of the linen and the other to the wrong side of the lining fabric.

10. On the back of the flap lining piece, reinforce the place where the other half of the magnetic clasp will go with a small piece of lightweight interfacing (such as Decovil I Light) – centrally, about 2cm (³/₄in) up from the bottom edge. Attach the other half of the clasp (see page 14).

11. With the right sides together, sew the fused linen section to the lining piece leaving the top (flat) edge open.

12. Trim the seam allowance back leaving a double seam allowance on the top (flat) edge. Clip the curves and turn the right way out. Topstitch in an appropriate thread colour very close to the edge.

13. Sew the crocheted flower and button on over the top of the magnetic clasp.

14. Sew along the top edge of the flap very close to the edge to close it. Site the flap 2cm (³/₄in) above the pocket – it is actually more important that the magnetic clasp closes neatly so let that be your guide. Fold the sewn and trimmed top edge under and attach the pocket flap to the backpack front with a double row of topstitching.

80

The back

15. Make the back exactly the same way as the front, but without a pocket, and make the bottom panel a little shorter: it measures 16.5cm x 41cm (6¹/₂ x 16in). Be very sure about measuring. When you come to sew on your linen trim, ensure that the strip will match up exactly when you put the front and back pieces together with the top edges aligned – it should travel around the bag without a step.

16. The back has a special section on the bottom (refer to image opposite), which will be prepared now and then attached later on. This is where the straps will attach. Sew your 8 x 41cm (3¹/₄ x 16in) coordinating strip to a piece of foam interfacing with a narrow seam. That's it for now!

The flap

17. Using the main flap template, cut two pieces from lightweight interfacing (such as Decovil I Light) and one piece from wadding/batting. Cut a piece of linen 33 x 20cm (13 x 8in) and a piece of lining the same size. Fuse a piece of lightweight interfacing to the wrong side of the flap lining and the linen. Fuse the piece of wadding/batting over the interfacing on the back of the linen. Centre all of these well.

18. Attach the male half of the magnetic clasp centrally, 1.5cm (³/₄in) up from the bottom of the flap lining (see page 14).

19. Place the two flap pieces right sides together and line up the interfacing, feeling your way. Sew around the curve leaving the straight top edge open.

20. Clip the curves and turn the right way out. Topstitch with coordinating thread. Sew the other flower on top of the magnetic catch, using the button to decorate the centre.

The straps and tabs

The straps measure 10 x 80cm (4 x 31½in) each; the tabs are each 10 x 15cm (4 x 6in). It is easier to make the whole length in one go and then cut. Depending on the size of the user, the straps and tabs may be shortened or lengthened.

Tip

Usually, Bundfix tape is my go-to for straps, but on a backpack it can be a bit more comfortable to have a slightly wadded strap. There isn't any magic involved with this though – simply make it up as you would normally.

21. Cut the fabric for the tabs and straps: 10 x 190cm (4 x 75in). Also cut a strip of wadding/batting 190cm (75in) long and 3.5cm (1½in) wide.

22. Enclose the wadding/batting inside the fabric, hiding all raw edges, and pin in place. Topstitch once along each side and three times up the centre.

23. Cut the strip to create your two 15cm (6in) long tabs, and two 80cm (31½in) long straps.

24. In each of the tab strips, thread through a rectangle ring, fold over and stitch to secure the ring in place.

25. On the bottom of the back of the bag, with right sides facing, sew a tab to each side, 7cm (2¾in) in from each side. Take the extra fabric strip that you made in step 16 and sew it onto the bottom so that the bag back is complete. Press.

The lining

26. Cut your two main pieces of lining fabric, 41 x 38cm (16 x 15in).

27. Make a couple of patch pockets, each 15 x 21cm (6 x 8¼in); see page 31. Attach one to each piece of lining fabric and sew some vertical divisions as needed. Use fusible interfacing (such as S320) to keep the pockets beautifully crisp.

Tip

To ensure the pockets are convenient, don't place them too deep in the bag. Think about what you need them for and custom-make them.

Putting it all together

28. Place the outer pieces right sides together and pin very carefully, lining up everything well. Sew the sides and base.

29. Cut 4cm (1½in) squares out of the corners and box them (see page 25). Turn the right way out.

30. Pinch the edges very narrowly from the top edge of the bag down to the linen trim and sew a narrow seam to help define the edge (see opposite). Repeat for the other three.

31. Cut a piece of foam board 30 x 9cm (12 x 3½in) and a piece of spare foam interfacing (if you have a bit) the same size. This measurement is a starting point. You will need to trim back so that it fits well. Hot glue the base into the bag and then glue the foam interfacing on top of it.

32. Fit the other half of the second magnetic clasp on the front of the bag. Measure down 10cm (4in) from the front centre top and install the female half. Don't forget to reinforce behind the clasp with a scrap of lightweight interfacing first.

33. Attach the straps by threading them through the sliders and then crossing them over at the middle top of the bag (refer to image on page 81). There will be a slight angle to be trimmed away – this makes them more comfortable to wear. Sew in place.

34. Sew on the flap, right sides facing the back of the bag and aligning the raw edges, making sure that it fits well with the magnetic snap on the front. Again, some trimming is nearly always necessary.

35. The lining is next. With right sides together, sew around the sides and bottom of the lining pieces, leaving a gap in the bottom edge for turning through. As in step 29, box the corners with 4cm (1½in) squares.

36. With the lining still inside out, pull it on over the bag so that the right sides are together. Sew around the top edge and turn out through the gap. Stitch the gap closed and then topstitch around the top edge.

37. On the top edges, install a plastic snap fastener each side to keep them together (see opposite) – this gives extra security for the contents, but you can open them out if you need to have a good rummage.

Anna Lena

This bag is a confection of pink and lilac and the most delicate green – perfect for your favourite little girl!

Finished size: 27 x 20 x 5cm ($10^2/_3$ x 8 x 2in), plus handle

The embellishment

1. Use the large heart, the small heart, the flower and the circle templates to make a stacked heart motif for the front of the bag. The small heart is made from your binding fabric (D), the flower is medium pink felt and the circle is light pink felt; finish the large turquoise felt heart with pinking shears to give a scalloped edge.

2. Stack them up in order and glue. Machine embroider around each motif except the turquoise heart. Sew the small green flower button to the centre.

The front

3. Make the front pocket first. Using the pocket template, cut a piece of green striped fabric C for the pocket outer, a piece of wadding/batting and a piece of lining. Also cut a piece of straight binding from your lilac floral (D) 31cm ($12^1/_4$in) long, and a piece of woven ribbon 5cm (2in) long.

4. Lay the lining face down, put the wadding/batting on top and the green striped fabric face up. Tack/baste the three layers together by hand and trim if needed. Bind the top edge, tucking the folded piece of lilac woven ribbon into the binding as you go (see page 28). I positioned my ribbon to the right-hand side of the bag.

5. Finish the binding on the back and then appliqué the heart motif to the centre of the pocket, embroidering around the edge of the turquoise heart layer to secure it.

6. Cut a piece of striped fabric B to 38 x 15cm (15 x 6in) and a piece of pink fabric A to 38 x 10cm (15 x 4in) and sew them together with the pink on the bottom; press. Place the template on the top, lining up the points on the pattern with the seam. Cut out the bag shape.

7. Cut a pink band from fabric A using the template. Sew that to the top of the bag.

8. Pin the pressed bag front to a piece of wadding/batting just slightly larger all around. Topstitch either side of the band and base seams. Lay the bound pocket on, matching up the landmarks on the pattern and sew it on the sides.

9. Cover the trimmed but raw bottom edge of the pocket with a piece of green ric-rac followed by a piece of lilac woven ribbon; sew, leaving just the scalloped edge of the ric-rac showing.

10. Trim as needed and then pin to a piece of foam interfacing just slightly larger than the bag front. Attach by sewing all around with a half-normal seam.

11. Cut out the darts and sew them, right sides facing.

Gather these supplies

Fabrics
- A: 1 fat quarter candy pink fabric, for bag outer and strap
- B: 1 fat quarter pretty striped fabric, for central bag panels, front and back
- C: 1 fat quarter green striped fabric, for pocket front
- D: 1 fat eighth lilac floral fabric, for binding
- E: 40cm (15¾in) strip of bright blue fabric, for linings

Interfacings
- 30cm (12in) strip foam interfacing (such as Style-Vil)
- 30cm (12in) strip dense quilt wadding/batting (such as Thermolam)
- 1 fat eighth fusible interfacing (such as S320)
- Bundfix tape, 7cm (2¾in) wide

Everything else
- Scraps of turquoise, medium and light pink felt
- Small green flower button
- 70cm (27⅔in) lilac woven ribbon
- 70cm (27⅔in) green jumbo ric-rac
- 18cm (7in) purple zip
- 2 plastic snap fasteners
- Scrap of ribbon for the zip pull
- Coordinating threads for topstitching
- Scalloped pinking shears
- Glue
- Your usual sewing needs

The back

12. Cut a piece of striped fabric B to 38 x 15cm (15 x 6in) and a piece of pink fabric A to 38 x 10cm (15 x 4in) and sew them together with the pink on the bottom; press. Lay the template on the top, lining up the points on the pattern with the seam. Cut out the bag shape.

13. Cut out a pink top band from fabric A using the template. Sew that to the top of the bag back and press.

14. Make the zip pocket by cutting a 25cm (10in) square of lining fabric E. Measure halfway down the back panel of the bag and crease it to mark. Draw a zip box with angled cutting lines measuring 1 x 18cm ($^3/_8$ x 7in) right on the centre crease. Make the zip box and install the zip with a topstitch (see pages 22–23).

15. Bring the long piece of lining up to complete the pocket – you only have to sew the sides of the lining as the top and bottom of the zip pocket will be caught in the seams.

16. Lay the pressed back section onto a piece of wadding/batting, pin and topstitch either side of the top seam (band/pocket section seam).

17. Trim the bottom of the striped section with ric-rac and then with woven ribbon. Make sure that the zip pocket lining is nice and flat when you do these last two steps and it will now be closed top and bottom.

18. Trim the wadding/batting and lay the bag back onto a piece of slightly larger foam interfacing. Attach with a half normal seam and then trim the foam interfacing back.

19. Cut and sew the darts.

20. Tie the scrap of ribbon through the zip pull.

The strap

21. Cut a piece of Bundfix tape 50cm (20in) long and a piece of pink fabric A the same length and 10cm (4in) wide. Fuse the tape to the back of the fabric. Cut a piece of woven ribbon the same length and stitch it down the length of the strap to one side of the fabric.

22. Fold in the raw edges of the strap fabric and then fold the piece in half using the perforations as a guide. Topstitch down both sides of the strap (see page 33).

> *Tip*
>
> Don't forget that the strap can be lengthened or shortened depending on the height of the user.

The lining

23. Using the template, cut two bag lining pieces from fabric E and two lining top bands from fabric C. Attach a band to the top of each lining piece; press.

24. Make two lined patch pockets, 13 x 10cm (5 x 4in), from fusible interfacing and the pink outer fabric A (see page 31).

25. Attach one to each piece of lining in the middle, 5cm (2in) down from the top.

> *Tip*
>
> Remember the vertical central crease trick when placing the pockets.

26. Make some vertical seams to divide the pockets.

27. Cut the darts on each piece and sew them.

Putting it all together

28. Place the bag front and back outers together with right sides facing. Make sure that you line up all of the trims and details perfectly. Sew the front and back together around the sides and bottom edge.

29. Do the same with the lining pieces, but this time leave a gap in the base for turning out.

30. Attach the strap to the outer bag, sewing securely at each end, right sides together with raw edges aligned.

31. Pull the inside-out lining on over the bag outer (so the right sides face) and sew around the top. Turn out through the gap in the lining and then close the gap. Stuff the lining down into the bag and topstitch the very top edge to keep it neat.

32. Add a plastic snap fastener to the centre pocket, just above the heart motif, and on the centre top edge.

Margaret

In our busy and hectic lives, what a joy it is to find a bag happy to do two jobs! This is the one that you've been looking for – it is a tote and a shoulder bag with a detachable strap. You'll aways be prepared in case you buy more than you intended at the shops...

Finished size as folded bag: 42 x 33 x 6cm (16½ x 13 x 2½in), plus strap

Finished size as tote bag: 42 x 49 x 6cm (16½ x 19¼ x 2½in), plus handles

The front

1. Using the triangle template, cut 14 triangles from the fat eighths for the front of the bag. To save time, cut the same number of triangles for the back of the bag and put them aside.

2. Sew the front 14 triangles together to make two rows of seven, with a good mix of colours and patterns (see page 21). Sew the two rows of seven first, then sew the two rows together to make the panel. Press. Trim the side triangles to make a rectangular panel that measures 47 x 28cm (18½ x 11in).

3. Cut a piece of fabric A to 18.5 x 47cm (7¼ x 18½in) and attach it, right sides together to the top of the triangle panel. Press.

4. Cut a second piece of fabric A to 10 x 47cm (4 x 18½in) and attach it to the bottom. Press.

5. Lay the patched and pressed panel over the top of the wadding/batting (which should be slightly larger) and pin together. Quilt with a vertical wavy pattern, then trim the wadding/batting back.

Gather these supplies

Fabrics
- A: 45cm (17¾in) grey patterned, for the front and back top and bottom panels
- B: 1m (1yd) coordinating pattern, for lining
- Fat eighths of six different grey, pink and purple fabrics
- C: fat eighth pink patterned, for the interior patch pockets
- D: 25cm (10in) grey patterned, for the strap, handles and tab detailing

Interfacings
- 1m (39½in) dense quilt wadding/ batting (such as Thermolam)
- 1m (39½in) fusible woven interfacing (such as G740)
- 1 fat quarter fusible interfacing (such as S320)

Everything else
- 2.4m (2⅔yd) grey webbing, 3cm (1¼in) wide
- 2 3cm (1¼in) silver 'D'-rings
- 1 3cm (1¼in) bag slider
- 2 3cm (1¼in) silver swivel clips
- 18cm (7in) pink zip
- 1 grey plastic snap fastener
- Your usual sewing needs

Here is the list of Art Gallery Fabrics I used, in case you want to use the same:

- A: + Your Heart Timid
- B: Uncaged Words Linen
- C: Petal Flamingoes Coo
- D: Cheshire Feathers Pastry

The back

6. Make the back bag panel the same as for the front, following steps 1–5.

7. Cut two pieces of pocket lining 28cm wide x 25cm deep (11 x 10in). Mark and then install a zip box 4cm (1½in) down from the top of the geometric panel in the centre; the box should measure 1 x 18cm (⅜ x 7in). The pocket lining top should sit flush with the top of the geometric panel. Sew the lining pieces together all round to complete the pocket lining (see pages 22–23 for more detail).

The adjustable strap, handles and tabs

These are made from webbing with a central trim of 2cm (¾in) wide straight binding, made from fabric D. The adjustable strap is 120cm (47½in) long, the two handles are each 50cm (20in) long and the tabs are each 10cm (4in) long. However, the handle size is not written in stone! If you are petite you can shorten them. Once constructed, stand with the tote in your hand and see how near the ground it is. You don't want it to skim the floor, so shorten the handles until you are happy.

8. Cut the pieces from webbing strap and make straight binding from fabric D to match the lengths (see page 28).

9. Attach the straight binding to the webbing in the dead centre (some double-sided tape helps here) and then sew along both long sides with matching thread.

10. The tabs enclose a 'D'-ring and are then sited at the top of the geometric panel on each side. The handles are attached front and back 13cm (5¼in) in from each side. Sew them all in place, right sides facing, with a narrow seam.

11. To make the adjustable strap, attach one end to the middle bar of the bag slider. Bring the other end through one of the swivel clips, back through the bag slider and then attach the free end to the remaining swivel clip.

The lining

12. Cut two pieces of fabric B to 46 x 53cm (18$\frac{1}{4}$ x 21in) and two pieces of woven interfacing (such as G740) the same size. Fuse the interfacing to the back of the fabric pieces.

Tip

We don't usually interface the lining because most of the rigidity comes from the bag outer. But because this bag has to fold over, we cannot use a foam interfacing. Therefore, a small amount of extra welly in the lining keeps it all crisp and the bag will fold without sticking out.

13. Make two lined patch pockets measuring 25 x 15cm (10 x 6in), using fusible interfacing (such as S320), lining fabric and pocket fabric C (see page 31).

14. Find the vertical centre of a lining piece and measure up 18cm (7in) from the bottom. Topstitch a patch pocket in place around the sides and bottom edge at this point. Repeat this for the other lining piece. Add a vertical line of stitching in the centre to stop the pockets sagging.

15. With the right sides together, sew the lining pieces together along the sides and bottom, but leave a turning gap in the bottom. Box the bottom corners by measuring a 3cm (1$\frac{1}{4}$in) square out of each, cutting it out and then pinching and sewing the corners (see page 25).

Putting it all together

16. Place the front and back sections of the bag right sides together and sew the sides and base leaving no gaps.

17. Box the corners by measuring a 3cm (1$\frac{1}{4}$in) square on each, cutting it out and then pinching and sewing the corners.

18. Turn the bag out the right way and the lining inside out and pull the lining on over the outer. Line the top seams up and pin. Sew around the top. Turn out through the gap in the lining and then sew the gap closed.

19. Stuff the lining down into the bag and topstitch around the top edge.

20. Finish by adding a grey plastic snap fastener in the top centre.

Here is the list of Art Gallery Fabrics I used, in case you want to use the same:

- A: Timber Nightfall
- B: Luna Rising Shadow
- C: In the Thicket Dusk
- D: Capped Dim
- E: Wild Posy Flora
- F: Maple Mill Fog
- G: Nocturnal
- H: Moonbeam

Christa

This bag celebrates gorgeous owls and wonderful woodlands. It combines both with an appliqué design that looks beautifully accomplished but is actually very easy to achieve.

Finished size: 47 x 38cm (18½ x 15in), plus handles

The appliqué owl pocket

1. Cut a 31cm (12¹/₄in) square of fabric A. Cut a piece of wadding/batting just slightly larger. Lay the fabric on top and tack/baste around the edge.

2. Use the templates to cut the owl appliqué pieces and cut them from the following fabrics:

The owl appliqué list

The face (1): natural linen
The wing (2): fabric H
Tail feather (3): fabric C
Main body (4): fabric F
Leaves (5): fabric E

3. Construct the owl shape from your fabric pieces and glue it onto the fabric square, roughly in the centre. Use the water-soluble marker to transfer details to the owl and also draw in the branch, using the template as a guide.

4. Set your machine up for FME and use black thread. Embroider the details on and anchor the owl down to the fabric at the same time. When you are happy with your embroidery, snip away any loose threads. Finish the pocket by trimming the wadding/batting back and cutting a 31cm (12¹/₄in) square of lining fabric (D). Find the centre top of the lining and reinforce the back with a 6cm (2¹/₂in) square of lightweight interfacing (such as Decovil I Light). Attach the female half of the magnetic clip to the lining (see page 14).

Tip

Don't be overwhelmed by the look of this owl. It isn't difficult and you have all of the details on the template. Simply copy them onto the appliqué and then 'draw' over them one, two or three times.

5. Place the lining wrong sides together with the appliquéd pocket front and tack/baste all around.

6. Make some straight binding from fabric G. You need enough to go across the top of the front pocket (at least 31cm/12¹/₄in; see page 28). Trim the top edge of the pocket with the binding.

Gather these supplies

Fabrics
- A: 1 fat quarter tree print, for the front pocket
- B: 50cm (½yd) coordinating fabric, for the bag back and inner pockets
- C: 40cm (15¾in) coordinating fabric, for the handles and zip tab
- D: 1m (1yd) coordinating fabric, for linings
- E, F, H: 1 fat eighth each of coordinating fabric, for appliqué
- G: 1 fat eighth coordinating fabric, for binding
- 60cm (23⅔in) charcoal melange linen, for the main bag body and front flap
- Scrap of natural linen, for the owl's face

Interfacings
- 60cm (23⅔in) dense quilt wadding/batting (such as Thermolam)
- Scraps of lightweight fusible interfacing (such as Decovil I Light)
- 2m (79in) foam interfacing (such as Style-Vil)
- 1 fat quarter fusible interfacing (such as S320)
- Scrap of woven fusible interfacing (such as G740)
- Bundfix tape, 7cm (2¾in) wide

Everything else
- Glue stick
- Black thread
- Water-soluble marker
- Medium silver magnetic clip
- Silver rectangle rings to suit the width of the webbing
- 18cm (7in) navy zip
- 25cm (10in) navy zip
- 61cm (24in) navy zip (slightly heavier)
- A couple of silver woodland inspired charms and some split rings and lobster clips with which to attach them
- 2m (79in) dark grey or navy strap webbing (about 3cm/1½in wide)
- Coordinating threads for topstitching
- 5 x 7cm (2½ x 2¾in) cotton tape
- Stamp
- Black ink
- Your usual sewing needs

The bag front

7. Cut a piece of linen, 52 x 40cm (20$\frac{1}{2}$ x 15$\frac{3}{4}$in). Cut a piece of wadding/batting slightly larger all round. Lay the wadding/batting down and put the linen on top, right side up. Mark the vertical centre of the linen and place the owl pocket on the centre line, 6cm (2$\frac{1}{2}$in) up from the bottom. Tack/baste the pocket on and tack/baste the linen to the wadding/batting.

8. Cut another piece of linen, 30 x 7cm (12 x 2$\frac{3}{4}$in). Lay it over the bottom of the pocket edge with the right side of the linen to the right side of the pocket, and sew along the bottom edge. Fold the linen down and press. Topstitch along the edge of the linen. This effectively takes care of the bottom raw edge of the pocket.

9. Fuse a piece of lightweight interfacing (such as Decovil I Light) onto the back of the wadding/batting and install the male half of the magnetic clasp so that it aligns with the female part already in your pocket.

10. Install a box zip measuring 18 x 1cm (7 x $\frac{3}{8}$in), 2.5cm (1in) down from the top of the bag. This will be hidden under the flap. The lining is a piece of fabric (D) 25cm wide by 50cm deep (10 x 20in). The top of the pocket lining will sit flush with the top edge of the bag (see pages 22–23).

11. Make the flap using the template. Draw it onto a piece of fusible interfacing (such as S320) and cut out accurately. Fuse the interfacing piece to the wrong side of a piece of linen that is larger all around.

12. Cut out a piece of lining the same size as the linen. With the right sides together, pin the interfaced linen to the lining.

13. Sew around the flap leaving the long flat edge open. Clip the curves and trim the seam allowance back and turn the right way out. Press and topstitch the sides and bottom edge narrowly with coordinating thread.

14. Site the flap dead centre, with the flat edge flush with the top of the bag. Stitch along the top edge. (The raw edge will be taken up when the lining goes in and a topstitch will stop the flap from sticking up – this is all done at the end of construction.)

15. Stamp your chosen print onto your label and fold it in half.

16. Cut two 44cm (17$\frac{1}{2}$in) lengths of webbing. Fold one end of each over, trapping a rectangle ring in the end. Tuck the cut end under and attach the strap to the left-hand side of the pocket, hiding the raw pocket edge. The strap comes to just over the top edge of the owl pocket. Repeat for the right-hand side, trapping the raw edges of your label under as you sew to secure it in place.

17. Find the centre bottom and mark it. Measure out 20cm (8in) either side of the mark and make another mark.

18. The top edge measures 50cm (20in). Go to the top corners of the bag and, with a ruler, draw a line from the very top edges to the marks that you made on the bottom. Cut along these lines to form an inverted trapezoid shape to the bag.

19. Lay the bag front, right side up, onto a slightly larger piece of foam interfacing; attach with a narrow seam and trim.

The back

20. Cut a piece of patterned fabric B, 35 x 33cm (14 x 13in). Cut a piece of linen 35 x 7cm (14 x 2³/₄in). Attach the strip of linen to the bottom of the patterned fabric (as you did for the bottom of the owl pocket on the front. This will extend the fabric panel but, more importantly, it matches the front piece, which will be important when everything is put together.

21. Cut two pieces of linen, 40 x 10cm (15³/₄ x 4in), and join one to each side of this central panel.

22. Lay the whole panel onto a piece of slightly larger wadding/batting, and pin the edges.

23. Find the dead centre and site a zip pocket 5cm (2in) down from the top edge. The pocket lining measures 27 x 65cm (10¹/₂ x 25³/₄in) (fabric D) and the box measures 1 x 25cm (³/₈ x 10in) (see pages 22–23). The zip pocket lining sits flush with the top edge of the bag.

24. Cut two pieces of webbing exactly the same as the front, and tuck a rectangle ring under the top end and stitch it on. Repeat for the other piece.

25. Cut the back piece to the same shape as the front, and attach it to a piece of foam interfacing with a narrow seam. Trim.

26. Before you sew the front and back pieces together, use one of them as a template for the lining pieces. Cut two pieces of lining.

27. Place the outer back and front pieces of the bag together with right sides facing and pin (trim if necessary). Sew around the sides and bottom leaving no gaps. Clip across the bottom corners to reduce bulk.

The zip top

28. Begin by choosing a fabric to make a tab (I used fabric C). Cut a piece of fabric 5.5 x 13cm (2^1/$_4$ x 5in) and interface it with woven interfacing (such as G740).

29. Fold it in half, right sides facing, and sew up the sides to make a little bag. Trim the seam allowance back a bit and turn the right way out. Fold the raw ends in (there is plenty to play with and you can trim this). Slip the tab onto the open end of the zip. Topstitch a square to secure it to the zip.

30. With right sides facing, pin the zip in place along the top edge of the bag, starting 1cm (3/8in) away from the seam on the left-hand side (the opening end) and pinning to 1cm (3/8in) away from the right-hand side (the closed end).

> ### Tip
> This is a simple way of adding a zip without a top gusset and the end will dangle outside the bag. The reason that there is a 1cm (3/8in) gap each end is to give some room for the lining, which will in turn hide the edges and zip ends.

31. On the left side, fold the zip tape ends up and away. They will be hidden in the lining. Sew the zip in.

Handles

32. Cut two pieces of Bundfix tape 70cm (27^2/$_3$in) long. Cut two pieces of fabric C the same length and 10cm (4in) wide. Fuse the Bundfix tape to the wrong side of the fabric so that the tape is in the middle and there is a bit of fabric clearance each side.

> ### Tip
> This Bundfix tape is magic stuff: depending on how you fold it, it can make three different strap widths! We are after 3.5cm (1^3/$_8$in) this time, so the tape is folded in half using the centre perforations and then the extra fabric is tucked under the long edge.

33. Fold the tape and fold the fabric in and iron it. Topstitch along the length five times to close the strap and to decorate and reinforce it. Trim the end.

34. Repeat for the other strap. The straps are now ready to attach at the end of construction.

Lining

35. Make two lined patch pockets to attach to your lining pieces (see page 31). Make a double one, 22 x 18cm (8^3/$_4$ x 7in) and 20 x 13cm (8 x 5in), and a single one, 20 x 13cm (8 x 5in), using the fusible interfacing (such as S320) as a base, with fabric B and lining. To make the double pocket, just make two lined pockets and then topstitch one to the other using a very narrow seam. Make divisions and then continue as normal.

36. Topstitch a pocket to each piece of lining; I attached the single pocket 9cm (3^1/$_2$in) from the top and the double pocket 6cm (2^1/$_2$in) from the top.

> ### Tip
> When you put the pockets on, don't forget that they are quite big and will be inclined to gape. Counteract this by making vertical divisions in them for your pen, phone or other items.

37. With the right sides facing, sew the lining pieces together around the sides and bottom edge, leaving a gap in the bottom for turning out.

Putting it all together

38. With the outer bag the right way out, pull the inside-out lining on so that the right sides are together. Tack/baste to make sure that the zip is in the right place and remember to keep the zip tape ends tucked in on the opening end. Sew around the top edge completely. Turn the bag out through the gap in the lining and then sew it closed.

39. Stuff the lining down into the bag and topstitch the top edge. Usually when you topstitch, you pull any flaps up and out of the way. Not this time! Topstitch straight over the front flap – this will help it to lie flat and not stick up.

40. Sew the handles to the rectangle rings.

41. Add some night-inspired bag charms: think owls and moons, that sort of thing, and join them together with some strong jump rings. Attach them to lobster clips and attach to the zip pulls.

> ### Tip
> Use over-sized lobster clips and heavy-duty jump rings so that they are nice and strong.

Here is the list of Art Gallery Fabrics I used, in case you want to use the same:

- A: Tropical Breeze
- B: Sand Bar in Canvas
- D: Afternoon Sail solid smooth denim
- E: Bouyant Vista in coral and Bouyant Vista in white
- F: Trade Winds Harbour
- G: Sparkler Flare

Ingrid

Packing a beautiful bag can get you in the mood for a holiday. This one is the perfect size for a weekend away, with lots of practical pockets and a roomy interior. And it is much easier than it looks to make. You might well end up booking a holiday just to show it off!

Finished size: 57 x 41 x 12cm (22½ x 16 x 4¾in), plus handles or strap

The straps

There are two sets of straps: handles that are permanently fixed to the bag and a removable, adjustable shoulder strap.

1. The handles are made from fabric A. Cut a piece of Bundfix tape 140cm (55¼in) long and cut a piece of fabric 10cm (4in) wide and as long as the tape. Fuse the tape centrally to the wrong side of the fabric, fold the raw edges in and then fold in half using the perforations as a guide. Topstitch along both sides twice and then cut the strap in half to make two handles (see page 33).

2. To make the adjustable strap, cut 130cm (51¼in) of Bundfix tape. Cut the same amount of fabric B, 10cm (4in) wide. Fuse the tape centrally to the wrong side of the fabric, fold the raw edges in and then fold in half using the perforations as a guide. Topstitch along both sides twice.

3. Attach one end of the strap to the bag slider and secure. Bring the other end through a swivel clip, back through the bag slider and then affix to the other swivel clip. The strap is now ready to attach to the 'D'-rings that will later be enclosed in the tabs at each end of the zip.

The lining

The lining for this bag is not the usual drop-in style. It is fitted to each panel and then the raw edges inside the bag are bound with bias tape. The benefit to using this method is a nice tight and fitted lining, which cannot sag. Make each lining panel and then tack/baste to the back of the corresponding outer one.

4. The large front and back lining pieces are the same – cut two pieces of lining fabric using the main bag template.

5. Cut two pieces of fusible interfacing (such as S320) each measuring 35 x 20cm (14 x 8in) to make patch pockets. The pocket fabric is fabric F, lined with fabric G. Make two lined patch pockets (see page 31).

6. Attach these to the lining pieces in the centre, about 12.5cm (5in) down from the top edge. You can adjust the distance a bit here to suit. Sew in vertical pocket divisions to prevent sagging – choose how wide to make the divisions based on what you will use them for.

7. Cut another piece of lining for the gusset measuring 105 x 14cm (41½ x 5½in).

Gather these supplies

Fabrics
- A: 1m (1yd) blue floral, for sides of front and back pockets, zip panel, handles and strap
- B: 1 fat quarter blue patterned, for centre of front and back pockets
- C: 50cm (½yd) navy solid, to make tabs and 5m (5.4yd) navy bias binding, see page 27
- D: 1m (1yd) blue, for main bag pieces
- E: 1m (1yd) coral patterned, and 40cm (15¾in) white patterned, for linings. If you prefer to have the lining all the same colour, simply add the measurements together
- F: 1 fat quarter blue patterned, for internal patch pockets
- G: 1 fat quarter white patterned, for internal patch pocket linings

Interfacings
- 2m (79in) foam interfacing (such as Style-Vil)
- 1m (39½in) 80/20 cotton mix sew-in wadding/batting (such as #279)
- 1 fat quarter fusible interfacing (such as S320)
- 50cm (20in) fusible wadding/batting (such as H630)
- 1m (39½in) heavy-duty interfacing (such as S133) for the base
- Bundfix tape, 7cm (2¾in) wide
- 1 fat quarter fusible interfacing (such as Decovil)

Everything else
- 1 71cm (28in) navy zip (open-ended and heavy duty)
- 2 navy 18cm (7in) zips
- 4 large bag feet
- Ribbon scraps for the zip pulls
- Small 'D'-ring
- Large anchor charm
- 1 2cm (¾in) 'D'-ring
- 4cm (1½in) silver bag slider
- 2 medium silver swivel clips
- 2 4cm (1½in) silver 'D'-rings
- Coordinating threads for topstitching
- Your usual sewing needs

101

The front

8. Begin with the front pocket, which has three divisions and runs across the whole width of the bag. Using the template, cut the corner trims from interfacing (such as Decovil) – in total you need four of these, two for the front pocket and two for the back pocket, and remember that they have to be mirror images! Cut all four at once and be done with it. Fuse each of these to the wrong side of some denim fabric. Trim back to the interfacing on each side except the large inner curve – here you should allow about 1cm (3/8in) extra fabric. Clip into the curve and then fold the fabric back over the interfacing. A small amount of double-sided tape will keep everything in place.

9. For the front pocket, cut the following:

The front pocket cutting list

1 piece of fabric B: 22 x 28cm (8¾ x 11in) for the middle

2 pieces of fabric A: 20 x 28cm (8 x 11in) for either side

1 piece of lining fabric: 60 x 28cm (23²/₃ x 11in)

A piece of straight navy binding: 57cm (22½in) long

10. Join the centre and side pieces of fabric together.

11. Lay the pocket front onto a piece of sew–in wadding/batting (such as #279) that is slightly larger all round and quilt with vertical wavy lines in a freeform meandering pattern.

12. Trim the pocket wadding/batting to the same size as the front. Using a water-soluble marker, draw the outline of the large template onto the pocket so that the denim trims sit in the right place.

13. Taking the denim trims made in step 8, place one in each of the bottom corners and use a coordinating thread to topstitch them on with a narrow seam.

14. Place the lining and the pocket front wrong sides together and bind the top edge with navy straight binding (see page 28). As you sew, attach a piece of ribbon with the small 'D'-ring into the binding. This will be used to hang the anchor charm later on. I positioned the charm slightly left of centre, but choose where you want yours to sit.

15. Using the template lines that you drew onto the pocket, trim it to the proper curved shape. Tack/baste the three pocket layers together for stability.

16. Use the large template to cut a bag front from fabric D. Lay it onto a piece of untrimmed sew-in wadding/batting (such as #279) and pin. With coordinating thread, quilt the panel with a horizontal wavy pattern (just let the machine meander in freeform waves). Trim the wadding/batting back to size.

17. Cut the two small zips down to 12cm (4³/₄in) long.

18. Find the vertical centre of the main panel and mark. Measure down 7cm (2³/₄in) and draw a box 12 x 1cm (4³/₄ x ³/₈in).

19. Cut a piece of pocket lining 18 x 36cm (7 x 14¼in). Insert the zip box; the zip pocket lining will be flush with the top of the bag (see pages 22–23). Finish with a scrap of ribbon through the zip pull.

20. Lay the front pocket onto the trimmed denim panel and tack/baste together.

21. To attach the straps, first find and mark the centre of each end. Feed the strap under the front pocket with the centre mark lining up exactly with the seams between your three fabric pieces. Feed each handle in by about 2.5cm (1in). Sew a rectangle around on the strap end to secure it.

22. Divide the front pocket into three sections with some vertical seams right on the fabric joins. Stitch in the ditch (within the existing seam) for this so that the seams are invisible; this will further reinforce your straps.

23. Lay the completed front onto a piece of slightly larger foam interfacing and attach with a narrow seam. Trim the foam back.

24. Attach a piece of lining back to back straight onto the foam with a tacking/basting stitch.

The back

25. Make the back exactly the same as the front but leave out the hanging ribbon and 'D'-ring for the charm. You now have a completed front and back with zip, lining and handles in both.

The top zip gusset

26. Cut two pieces of fabric A, two pieces of fusible wadding/batting (such as H630) and two pieces of lining, all to 71 x 7cm (28 x 2¾in). Fuse the wadding/batting pieces to the wrong side of the fabric A pieces.

27. Make a 'zip sandwich', attaching a piece of outer and lining to each side of the zip (see page 24).

28. From the navy solid fabric, make two tabs. Cut a piece of Bundfix tape 26cm (10¼in) long and a piece of navy solid the same size. Fuse the tape to the fabric, fold and topstitch with coordinating thread. Cut the tab strip in half and then fold each one in half, enclosing a 'D'-ring in each. These are the hanging tabs for the removable adjustable strap.

29. Attach a tab centrally to each end of the zip, sewing with right sides facing and raw edges aligned.

The base

30. Cut a piece of fabric D to 105 x 14cm (41$\frac{1}{2}$ x 5$\frac{1}{2}$in) and fuse to a piece of fusible wadding/batting (such as H630). Note that this measurement, like my other gussets, is rounded up. You can then fit and trim as needed. You cannot trim what you do not have!

31. Cut a piece of heavy-duty fusible interfacing (such as S133) 1cm (3/8in) smaller all around than the interfaced fabric. Find the centre of the interfaced fabric and base, and the centre of the heavy-duty interfacing and line the marks up. Fuse the heavy-duty interfacing to the wadded/batted side of the base.

Tip

This is really heavy stuff normally used for baseball cap peaks. Keep it out of the seam allowance for ease of putting it all together.

32. Attach the four bag feet to the bottom, 15cm (6in) from the centre and 3cm (1$\frac{1}{4}$in) in from the edges.

33. Attach to a piece of foam interfacing with a narrow seam and then trim. This will cover the backs of the bag feet and make the base feel luxe! Sew the lower gusset lining to the foam side of the base with the wrong sides together.

34. Attach each end of the base piece to the zip gusset, right sides together, to make a 'loop'.

Putting it all together

35. Attach the front panel of the bag to the gusset loop, right sides facing. Leaving the zip open, sew the back of the bag in place.

36. Bind the raw edges at the ends of the zip with navy bias binding. You will see that there are more raw edges. Simply turn the bag inside out and use the navy bias binding to bind them (see page 28). You may need to trim them a bit, but don't trim away too much because they need to be strong.

37. Turn the bag the right way out again and add the anchor charm to finish.

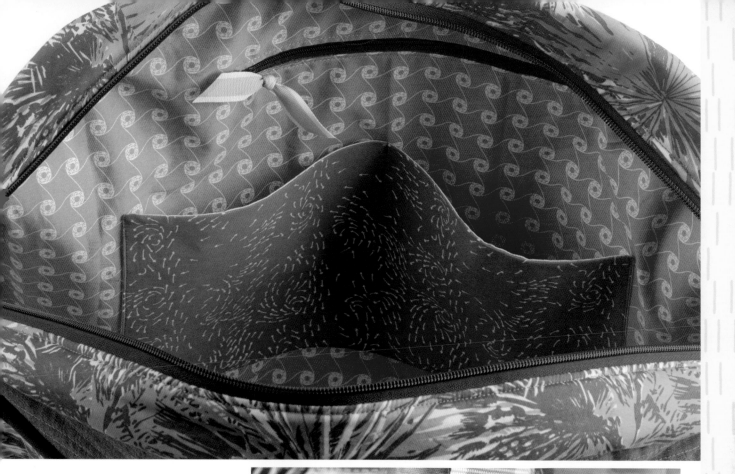

Ina

I think that the ultimate bag should not be too big and, of course, not too small. It should have pockets, and they shouldn't be too big or small either. Everything has to be just right: I really should have called this one the Goldilocks bag, but Ina was my lovely Nana's name, so that was the winning title!

Finished size: 28 x 32 x 8cm (11 x 12½ x 3¼in), plus strap

The front

1. Start by making the pocket flap. Using the template, cut a flap piece from fusible interfacing (such as S320) and fuse it to the back of a slightly larger piece of fabric A. Cut the lining to the same size as the fabric and then, with the right sides together, sew around the edges of the interfacing but leave the top flat edge open.

2. Trim and clip the corners and turn the flap the right way out. Press and then, when the edges are perfect, topstitch the edge with a narrow seam in a coordinating thread. Trim the long flat edge. Attach the female half of the twist lock to the middle bottom of the flap, about 1.5cm (²/₃in) up from the bottom.

3. Next make the lined patch pocket: from fusible interfacing (such as S320), cut a piece 23 x 16cm (9 x 6¼in). Fuse to the back of a slightly larger piece of fabric A and then add a scrap of the same interfacing to the back centre on the wrong side.

Tip

The scrap of fusible interfacing is to reinforce the back of the female half of the twist lock. This stops twisting and potential tearing with repeated opening.

4. Install the other half of the twist lock 5cm (2in) down from the top edge of the pocket, in the centre.

5. Cut a piece of lining to the same size as the pocket front. Put the two pieces right sides together and sew around, but this time, leave the entire bottom long end open. Turn the right way out, press and topstitch. Trim the bottom. You may actually find it easier – because the bottom is left open – to line the pocket first and then reach in from the bottom and install the lock. It is a bit bulky to sew around!

6. Cut a piece of fabric B to 31 x 21cm (12¼ x 8¼in) – this will sit behind the pocket. Cut a second piece of fabric B to 31 x 7cm (12¼ x 2³/₄in) for the bottom, and then a third piece to 31 x 10cm (12¼ x 4in) for the top. Fuse all pieces to wadding/batting (such as H630) the same size.

7. Make 126cm (49²/₃in) of piping with fabric D (see page 29). Cut it into four pieces – two for the front and two for the back.

8. To assemble the front, find and mark the vertical centres of all the elements. This will make it very easy to get everything perfect. Take the middle piece of fabric A first and lay the flap and pocket on top. The lock should close without wrinkles and puckering, and the top of the flap and the bottom of the pocket should be flush with the top and the bottom of the fabric piece. Adjust and trim as needed. Sew the top edge of the flap and the bottom and sides of the pocket to secure it.

Gather these supplies

Fabrics
- A: 50cm (½yd) blue cotton denim, for the gusset, front pocket, patch pockets and strap
- B: 50cm (½yd), purple floral, for the front and back
- C: 1m (1yd) pink patterned, for the lining
- D: 1 fat quarter lime, for the piping

Interfacings
- 1 fat quarter fusible interfacing (such as S320)
- 1m (39½in) foam interfacing (such as Style-Vil)
- Bundfix tape, 7cm (2¾in) wide
- 15cm (6in) square scrap of woven fusible interfacing (such as G740)
- 1m (39½in) fusible interfacing (such as S133 – this is a weird amount because you need only a narrow strip – trust me though, you will use this again! It is not quite wide enough to make the cut crosswise and you cannot join it for this exercise, as the join will be a visible weakness)
- 1 fat quarter fusible wadding/batting (such as H630)

Everything else
- 2 20cm (8in) zips, grey (back and front)
- 2 18cm (7in) zips, white (lining)
- 1 51cm (20in) grey zip (top zip) – heavier duty open-ended
- 1 medium silver twist lock
- 2 3.5cm (1³/₈in) silver rectangle rings
- 120cm (47½in) medium piping cord
- Coordinating threads for topstitching
- Label making materials – stamp, ink, Kraft-tex™ paper
- Beads for the zip pulls, and strong beading thread
- Your usual sewing needs

Here is the list of Art Gallery Fabrics I used, in case you want to use the same:
- A: Cool Foliage solid smooth denim
- B: He Loves Me Plum
- C: Chopsticks Rainbow
- D: Dark Citron

9. Sew piping to the top and bottom of the panel, with the raw edges aligned (see page 30).

10. Take the two extra pieces of fabric A – sew the smaller one to the bottom and the larger to the top, right sides facing. Topstitch under the piping on the bottom and over it on the top with a coordinating thread.

11. Cut two pieces of lining fabric 27cm wide by 20cm deep ($10^2/_3$ x 8in) and then make a zip pocket in the centre of the top panel, 4cm ($1^1/_2$in) down from the top (see pages 22–23). The zip box should measure 1 x 20cm ($^3/_8$ x 8in).

12. Round the bottom corners of the front (a cup works).

13. Press the front panel carefully and then attach to a piece of slightly larger foam interfacing with a half normal seam and then trim.

The back

14. The back is constructed very much the same way as the front, but instead of the large flap pocket, there is a box zip pocket. Begin by cutting the fabric panels. You will need:

The back panel cutting list

Fabric B, three pieces
- 21 x 31cm (8¼ x 12¼in) for the middle section
- 7 x 31cm (2¾ x 12¼in) for the bottom section
- 10 x 31cm (4 x 12¼in) for the top section

2 pieces of fabric C for the pocket lining: 25cm wide by 20cm deep (10 x 8in)

15. Fuse each of the fabric B pieces to wadding/batting (such as H630) the same size and then trim back if needed.

Tip

I have added a cute label under the zip pocket too. I chose a bee stamp because it went with the daisies, but it is up to you! Attach the label before you construct the back. It goes in the centre of the middle panel, about 4cm (1½in) down from the top.

16. Join the three interfaced panels together and add the piping as before (see step 9). Don't forget to topstitch above and below the piping as appropriate.

17. Construct the zip box pocket in the same way and the same position as the front zip pocket (see step 11). Centre it on the top panel as before.

18. Press and trim. Sew to a piece of foam interfacing with a narrow seam and then trim it back.

19. Make and add a little beaded charm to the zip pulls.

The top zip

25. Your top gusset pieces are 6cm wide by 32cm long ($2^1/_2$ x $12^1/_2$in) and there are four components: two outer pieces (fabric B) and two lining. You also need two pieces of wadding/batting (such as H630) the same size. Fuse the wadding/batting to the fabric B pieces.

26. Fold the ends of all four pieces of fabric in by 2cm ($^3/_4$in). (The sizes given are slightly longer than necessary: you want them to be easy to handle and there is nothing worse than fiddling with a bit of rapidly fraying end. You can always trim them back if you need to). Tack/baste the folded ends down for even easier handling. They need to be kept quite precise so that when they are topstitched in the final steps, they look super neat.

27. Take an outer piece, the zip and a lining piece and fold back the end tape (opening end) of the zip and line everything up and pin (you can tack/baste this too if you want to). You should have a zip sandwich with the two gusset pieces right sides together on the edge of the zip tape and the zip in the middle (see page 24).

28. Sew down along the zip. Unfold everything and press the right way out. Pin or tack/baste and then topstitch up one short side, along the zip and then down the other short side.

29. Sew in the other side of the zip in the same way.

The gusset

20. Cut a piece of denim, 10 x 92cm (4 x $36^1/_4$in) and fuse it to a piece of wadding/batting (such as H630). Cut a piece of interfacing (such as S133) to 8 x 90cm (3 x $35^1/_2$in) and fuse that centrally to the wadding/batting. Sew the gusset to a piece of foam interfacing with a narrow seam and then trim the foam.

The tabs

21. The two tabs are made from 20cm (8in) of Bundfix tape and a piece of denim 10cm (4in) wide by 20cm (8in) long. Fuse the tape centrally to the wrong side of the fabric, fold the raw edges in and then fold in half using the perforations as a guide. Topstitch along both sides twice. Cut the strap in half and enclose a ring in each piece.

The strap

22. To make the adjustable strap, cut two pieces of fabric, one denim and one fabric B, to 6cm ($2^1/_2$in) wide and 130cm ($51^1/_4$in) long. Sew them together along one long edge, right sides facing, then open out and press the seam open.

23. Cut a piece of Bundfix tape 130cm ($51^1/_4$in) long. Fuse it to the back, fold the fabric around it, concealing the raw edges, pin, then double topstitch to match the tabs (see page 33). Remember to use coordinating thread in the bobbin and top of the machine. They will be different.

24. Trim the end of the strap and secure one end to the middle bar of the bag slider. The rest will be done at the end.

Tip

These gusset sides are slightly wider than you need. Complete the zip and then fit onto the bag before trimming perfectly to fit. You don't want the zip to be pulling (gusset too small) and you don't want it to be raised up in the middle (gusset too big).

The zip tab

30. To make the tab for the end of the zip, cut a piece of fabric B to 5 x 15cm (2 x 6in) and interface with a scrap of woven interfacing (such as G740). Fold it in half and sew the sides down to make a little bag. Trim the seam allowance slightly and turn the right way out. Push the raw edges down into the bag to make a square. You have plenty to play with and you can trim it away if you like – I tend to leave it because it adds to the substance of the tab. The tab will be put onto the shortened end of the zip in the final steps and then topstitched on.

The lining

The lining is a bit different this time – there are two pockets each side: a zipped one with a lined patch pocket underneath! Double pockets are easy. You will make the zip pocket first (see pages 22–23) and then the only thing that you need to remember is to lift the pocket lining from the zip pocket up and out of the way before you topstitch the patch pocket on top (see page 31).

31. Cut two pieces of lining 29cm wide x 32cm deep (11$\frac{1}{2}$ x 12$\frac{1}{2}$in) and round the bottom corners on each as you did for the outer bag.

32. Cut a gusset piece 8 x 92cm (3$\frac{1}{8}$ x 36$\frac{1}{4}$in).

33. Find the vertical centre of both the front and back lining pieces and make a zip box pocket on each, following the method on pages 22–23. For each zipped pocket, the lining is cut 22cm wide x 40cm deep (8$\frac{3}{4}$ x 15$\frac{3}{4}$in). The zip boxes should sit 4cm (1$\frac{1}{2}$in) down from the top of the lining; the top of the pocket lining will be flush with the top edge of the bag.

34. Complete the zipped pockets and then lift the lining pieces up and out of the way.

35. For the patch pockets, cut two pieces of fusible interfacing (such as S320) to 20 x 15cm (8 x 6in). Cut a piece of lining slightly larger and a piece of outer the same as the lining. Fuse the interfacing to the wrong side of the outer and off you go (see page 31). Press after turning through.

36. Topstitch the lined patch pockets in place, 4cm (1$\frac{1}{2}$in) down from the zip pockets.

37. Make some vertical seam divisions in the patch pockets to prevent sagging.

38. Sew the front and back lining pieces to the gusset, right sides facing, and leave a sizeable gap in the bottom of the lining for turning out – the gap needs to be big enough to admit the whole bag, but do not go beyond the curved corners – these are difficult to close neatly afterwards.

Putting it all together

39. Attach the front and the back outer pieces of the bag with the gusset in the middle. I am not going to pretend that this is not a bit of a wrestle – the best way to do it is to tack/baste the gusset in – that way, you can make sure that it is not twisted and that it all fits together. Find the centre point at the bottom of both bag pieces and mark them. Find the centre of the gusset and then match these marks up. Begin attaching the gusset from the centre marks. You will see that there is extra at the top on both sides. You haven't done anything wrong! I always make the gusset longer... just in case. When it is in, trim the excess away.

40. Tack/baste a tab with a rectangle ring in it onto the front right-hand side, right sides facing, 4cm (1$\frac{1}{2}$in) in from the right edge, and to the corresponding opposite side on the back (you will leave the strap until the lining goes in).

41. The top gusset with the zip goes on next. Simply open the zip, taking advantage of the fact that it is an open-ended one, and place each side of the gusset with the lining facing up and the raw edge aligned with the top of the bag. Sew the gusset pieces in. Put the zip back together and shorten it to about 44cm (17$\frac{1}{2}$in), or the length of your choice. The very least that you should do is to make a new stop and cut the plastic bits off the end – they are too bulky.

42. Sew the little zip tab on the end of the zip by topstitching around the edge.

43. With the bag the right way out, slip it into the lining, which is inside out, so that the right sides of the outer and lining fabrics are touching. Pin the two sections together. Stitch around the top edge and then turn out through the gap in the lining. Stitch up the gap in the linings and push the lining down into the bag.

44. Topstitch the top edge of the bag. Topstitch along the zip gussets too. This topstitching not only looks decorative, it makes the bag strong too.

45. Attach the strap by taking it through a rectangle ring and then back through the slider. Take the free end of the strap through the other rectangle ring and secure.

Gertrude

This is a simple bag with minimal interfacings – ideal if you are just starting out in the world of bag making. It is perfect for a little girl who will love its bright appeal and the fact that it has lots of sections to keep all her treasures safe. Best of all, it has a cross-body strap so she won't get sick of carrying it around.

Finished size: 18 x 22 x 6cm (7 x 8¾ x 2½in), plus strap

The strap and tabs

1. The small hanging motif tab is made from a scrap of fabric C, around 8cm (3¼in) long. Make an open-ended tab and enclose the 'D'-ring inside; see page 33. Sew the ends together to keep them neat. Put aside until you are ready to make the middle angled pocket on the front.

2. The tabs that carry the strap are made from fabric A. Cut two pieces 10 x 5.5cm (4 x 2¼in). Fold the fabric in half lengthways, with the right sides together, and sew down the long side and across the bottom, leaving one short end open for turning. Trim the seam allowance and clip across the corners and then turn the right way out. Press so that the edges are perfect and trim the open end. Repeat for the other tab. Put these tabs to one side.

3. Cut the strap fabric 7cm wide and 1m long (2¾ x 39½in). Tuck in the raw edges, fold and then make a strap 2.5cm (1in) wide, topstitching with coordinating thread, once down each side (see page 33). Attach one end of the strap to the bag slider and then put it aside until the bag is finished.

The front

4. Use the template to cut the two angled front sections, the front from floral fabric (A) and the middle from the orange spot fabric (B). Also cut an entire front section from the secondary floral fabric (C).

5. Cut a piece of wadding/batting for the main bag front section slightly larger all round. Cut pieces of lining for the two angled sections (the main piece will be lined with the main lining inside the bag).

6. To make each angled pocket section, lay the outer fabric on top of the corresponding lining piece, wrong sides together and adjust to make sure all of the edges are perfect. Pin or tack/baste together. Sew the top edge and bind with bias binding (see page 28). When you come to sew the middle pocket's binding, don't forget that the small tab you created in step 1 needs to be inserted to take the hanging motif; position it about 5cm (2in) in from the right-hand edge.

7. Take the main fabric and lay it over the wadding/batting. Pin and attach with a narrow seam. (If you prefer fusible wadding/batting, you could use H640 instead.)

8. Trim the wadding/batting back to the same size as the fabric. Lay the middle angled pocket onto it and align the bottom edges. Now lay the other angled pocket over the top and align everything.

9. Pin and then tack/baste the pockets together in preparation for sewing. Sew the front section together around the sides and bottom.

Gather these supplies

Fabrics
- A: 1 fat quarter bright floral fabric, for the bottom front panel and the back of the bag
- B: 1 fat quarter spot fabric, for the middle of the bag and the patch pockets
- C: 30cm (12in) second floral fabric, for the top front and the straps
- D: 30cm (12in) striped fabric, for the lining

Interfacings
- 1 fat quarter 80/20 cotton wadding/batting (such as #279)

Everything else
- 2 2.5cm (1in) silver 'D'-rings
- 1 silver 2.5cm (1in) bag slider
- 1 2cm (¾in) silver 'D'-ring
- 1 plastic snap fastener
- Bias binding to coordinate
- 18cm (7in) zip
- Label for the back (see page 114)
- 14 x 6cm (5½ x 2½in) bag base mesh
- Hot glue gun
- Felt flower
- Slightly smaller crochet flower
- Round felt shape
- Cute button
- Scraps of ribbon
- Coordinating threads for topstitching
- Perle 8 coton in a colour to suit your fabric
- Fray stopper
- Your usual sewing needs

> ## Tip
>
> Because this bag is for a child, there is no interfacing in the pockets. It is a simpler make with only the main bag containing wadding/batting.

The lining

15. Cut two pieces of lining fabric using the template.

16. Make two unlined patch pockets from fabric B; mine are 9 x 15cm (3^1/$_2$ x 6in). Simply turn over a double hem on each side of the fabric, then topstitch in place on each of the lining pieces, about 5cm (2in) down from the top.

17. With the right sides facing, sew the lining pieces together around the sides and bottom, leaving a gap in the base.

18. Cut a 2.5cm (1in) square from each bottom corner of the lining and box the corners (see page 25).

Putting it all together

19. With the right sides facing, sew the bag outer back and front pieces together around the sides and bottom. Cut out a 2.5cm (1in) square from each bottom corner. Box the corners (see page 25).

20. Hot glue a trimmed piece of bag mesh into the base. Cut a scrap of wadding/batting and hot glue it over the bag mesh to make it feel softer.

21. With the outer the right way out and the lining inside out, pull the lining on over the outer, so that the right sides are facing. Sew around the top edge. Turn out through the gap and then stitch the gap closed.

22. Using the perle coton and an even running stitch, topstitch around the top of the bag to keep the lining down.

The back

10. The back section is formed of two pieces and there is a box zip pocket at the top. Begin by cutting a piece of your floral fabric (A), 22 x 20cm (8^3/$_4$ x 8in), and a piece of your spotted fabric (B), 22 x 6.5cm (8^3/$_4$ x 2^1/$_2$in). Sew the spotted top to the floral and press. Topstitch your label onto the bottom section of the bag.

11. To make the box zip pocket see pages 22–23. Cut a piece of lining 18cm wide x 36cm deep (7 x 14^1/$_4$in); the zip pocket lining will be flush with the top of the spotted panel. Mark a 1 x 16cm (^{3}/$_8$ x 6^1/$_4$in) zip box pocket 3cm (1^1/$_4$in) down on the vertical centre of the back panel. Install the zip pocket and then topstitch the zip in.

12. Bring the long end of the pocket lining up and pin it with the other short end flush with the top. Sew the sides and top to complete the pocket.

13. The zip has a small piece of ribbon through the pull. Pull the pocket lining up and out of the way.

14. Press the back panel and lay it onto a slightly larger piece of wadding/batting. Sew it on with a narrow seam allowance. Trim away any excess interfacing.

23. To attach the tabs created in step 2, slide on a D–ring, then tuck the back of the tab neatly behind the front, trimming if necessary and then pin and attach with a topstitch. I have put an X in the topstitch square too for decoration. Sew to the front left-hand side of the bag and also the rear left.

Tip

This will appear as the front left and the rear right when you are looking at the bag from the front.

24. Sew the strap to the tabs (see page 34).

25. Attach the plastic snap fastener to the middle top of the bag for a little extra security.

Embellishment

26. Sew the button to the small felt disc and then the crochet flower. Tuck an 8cm (3$\frac{1}{4}$in) length of ribbon through the 'D'-ring on the front of the bag, and then tuck it well behind the crochet flower and apply a dab of hot glue. Hot glue the crochet flower to the large felt one, ensuring that the ribbon is secure between the two. Finish with the other disc of felt on the back to hide any unfortunate bits.

Trixie

Little people love pretty things too, and they will be delighted with this handy and practical bag to carry their treasures around. This little bag is zip-free, so it is a great place to start!

Finished size: 20.5 x 24cm (8 x 9½in), plus handles

The front and back

The front and back pieces are made in the same way, but only the front has appliqué detailing.

1. Cut two pieces of green fabric B to 23 x 21cm (9 x 8⅜in) and two pieces of pink fabric A to 23 x 6cm (9 x 2½in).

2. Take a piece of green and a piece of pink and sew them together. Repeat for the other pink and green pieces.

3. On both the back and front pieces, attach the ric-rac along the horizontal fabric join. Attach the woven ribbon over the top.

4. Fuse the wadding/batting to the wrong side of the front and back panels.

Tip

Your sewing machine will appreciate the extra thickness as you appliqué the front panel: the fleece also keeps everything stable.

5. Using the template and your fabric scraps, cut a flower, a flower face and some leaves. Glue these onto the front panel of the bag.

6. Free-motion embroider the appliqué into place using blue thread. Trim away any thread ends and neaten.

7. Attach the aqua flower braid 2cm (¾in) down from the top edge on both the front and back pieces – make sure they are the same distance down, so that they will line up when the front and back pieces are put together. Sew a yellow flower button onto each braid flower.

8. Take 5cm (2in) of the cotton tape and 5cm (2in) of woven ribbon and sew the ribbon to the tape. Fold in half and make a tab; slide on the D-ring. Sew the tab in place, right sides facing, with a very narrow seam; position it on the left-hand side of the bag, 2cm (¾in) down from the top.

Gather these supplies

Fabrics
- A: 25cm (10in) pretty pink fabric, for top band and handles
- B: 1 fat quarter bright green fabric, for main bag outer
- C: 30cm (12in) strip bright pink spotted fabric, for lining

Interfacings
- 30cm (12in) strip fusible wadding/ batting (such as H640)
- 1 fat eighth fusible interfacing (such as S320)
- Bondfix tape, 7cm (2¾in) wide

Everything else
- 50cm (20in) light pink jumbo ric-rac
- 50cm (20in) aqua flower braid
- 50cm (20in) aqua and pink woven ribbon
- 20 yellow flower-shaped buttons
- Turquoise thread for appliqué
- Scraps of coordinating fabrics for the appliqué
- Large scraps of pink, green and yellow felt. Make one of these a thick piece for the back circle
- Yellow stranded embroidery thread
- Coordinating thread for topstitching
- 2cm (¾in) silver trigger clasp
- 2cm (¾in) silver 'D'-ring
- 20cm (8in) cotton tape (just a bit wider than your woven ribbon)
- Glue
- Water-soluble marker
- Scalloped pinking shears
- Your usual sewing needs

117

The handles

9. Cut two strips of fabric A, 10 x 41cm (4 x 16in); cut two lengths of Bundfix to 41cm (16in). Fuse the Bundfix tape to the wrong side of the handle strips.

10. Make two open-ended straps using the steps on page 33. Channel quilt a couple of times for comfort and strength.

The lining

11. Cut two lining pieces (fabric C), 23 x 26cm (9 x 10^1/$_4$in). Make two little lined patch pockets – about 10 x 10cm (4 x 4in) – using a piece of fusible interfacing (such as S320) to interface (see page 31).

12. Attach your patch pockets to the lining pieces. Site them in the middle, about 6cm (2^1/$_2$in) down from the top.

Putting it all together

13. Attach a handle to the front and back pieces: position the ends 4cm (1^1/$_2$in) in from each outer edge, with the right sides facing. With the handles against the right side of the fabric, pin a lining piece to each outer panel with the right sides together.

14. Sew along the top edge only. Repeat for the other side.

15. Open out and rearrange the pieces so that you align outer to outer and lining to lining, right sides facing. Sew all around the outer edge, but leave a gap in the lining.

16. Turn the right way out through the gap and sew it closed.

17. Push the lining down into the bag and topstitch around the top edge to keep the lining neatly in place.

The embellishments

18. Sew 15cm (6in) of woven ribbon to 15cm (6in) of cotton tape. Fold it in half, thread on the trigger clip and then sew the ends together.

19. Make the flower by cutting the shape from your pink felt, with a lemon felt centre, and glue it to an untrimmed piece of green felt. Decide which way is up and insert the hanging loop under the flower layers (it will be secured as you embroider).

20. Free-motion embroider the flower shape as you did the main appliqué. Carefully cut out the flower shape by trimming the green felt round with scalloped pinking shears.

21. Thread a needle with two strands of embroidery floss and make little sprays of straight stitches on each of the petals.

22. From the thick green felt, cut a circle just slightly larger than the scalloped one and glue the whole motif securely on. Put something heavy like a couple of textbooks on top of the motif until it is dry and it will be beautifully flat.

118

Sylvia

Another colour burst with lots of pretty details. Nothing beats this colour combination for impact! Plus it's versatile too: you could omit the strap and the charm and have a more subdued clutch.

Finished size: 20.5 x 12 x 4cm (8 x 4¾ x 1½in), plus strap

The front

1. Cut a front section using the template from the red and white fabric A. Fuse a piece of fusible wadding/batting (such as H630) the same size to the back.

2. Cut a piece of fusible interfacing (such as Decovil) to about 5 x 6cm (2 x 2½in) to reinforce the area where the clasp will sit. Fuse this to the wadding/batting side of the front, just up from the bottom. Attach the female half of the magnetic clasp set in the middle of the front section, 5cm (2in) up from the bottom (see page 14; the other half will go onto the flap).

3. Make the label: treat the ends of the cotton tape with fray stopper and stamp with your chosen image. Glue the label just above the magnetic clasp on the front piece, and secure with turquoise perle cotton and a running stitch. Sew the small green button to the top right-hand corner (refer to image on page 123).

Tip

This sweet idea gives you a reason to smile each time you open your bag.

---

4. Lay the front piece onto a slightly larger piece of foam interfacing and attach with a very narrow seam. Trim the foam back.

Gather these supplies

Fabrics
- A: 1 fat quarter red and white fabric, for the main bag body
- B: 40cm (15¾in) pretty turquoise and green fabric, for flap and strap
- C: 1 fat quarter red solid, for lining

Interfacings
- 1 fat quarter fusible wadding/batting (such as H630)
- 1 fat quarter foam interfacing (such as Style-Vil)
- 1 fat eighth fusible interfacing (such as Decovil)
- 1 fat eighth lightweight fusible interfacing (such as Decovil I Light)
- 1 fat eighth fusible interfacing (such as S320)
- Bundfix tape, 7cm (2¾in) wide

Everything else
- Scraps of felt or flower pre-cuts in red, green and turquoise
- 10cm (4in) red zip
- Glass beads for zip pull and charm
- Small silver spacer beads
- 2 25mm (1in) bronze 'D'-rings
- 1 bronze swivel clip
- 2 6mm (¼in) bronze cap rivets and setting tool
- 30mm (1¼in) bronze bag slider
- Small amount of woven ribbon in a coordinating colour
- White perle 8 cotton, turquoise perle 8 cotton
- Red and white spotted button
- Green button
- Crochet flower in red or turquoise – this can be self-made or you can buy them (layer a couple of colours up to get the right effect)
- Magnetic clasp
- Small green button
- 5 x 4cm (2 x 1½in) cotton tape
- Stamp and black ink
- Fray stopper
- Water-soluble marker
- Fabric glue stick
- Hot glue gun
- Sizzix Big Shot (if not using felt pre-cuts) and Sizzix flower dies (aim for sizes and shapes that will nest together)
- Your usual sewing needs

The back

5. Cut a red and white (fabric A) back piece using the same template and fuse it (wrong side again) to a piece of fusible wadding/batting (such as H630) the same size.

6. To insert the zip box pocket, see pages 22–23. Measure down 4cm (1^1/$_2$in) and draw a zip box, 9 x 1cm (3^1/$_2$ x ^{3}/$_8$in). Cut a piece of pocket lining 12cm wide and 25cm long (4^3/$_4$ x 10in). Insert the zip and then trim away the threads. Bring the long end of the lining up – the pocket lining will sit flush with the top of the back panel – and sew the sides and top of the pocket.

7. Make a little beaded charm by threading some matching beads onto the zip pull.

8. Lay the completed back onto a piece of foam interfacing and sew with a narrow seam. Trim the foam back.

The flap

9. Cut a flap piece from the turquoise fabric (B) and then fuse it to a piece of wadding/batting (such as H630) the same size. Cut a piece of lining too and a piece of lightweight interfacing (such as Decovil I Light) using the flap template, and put aside.

10. Arrange the three layers for your flower: the bottom one is turquoise, the next layer is red and green goes on the top. Glue the flower together and then stitch into place on the front of the flap, embellishing as you go with long stitches and some lazy daisy stitches, all using perle 8 cotton in white (see pages 35 and 37). The motif should sit 2.5cm (1in) up from the bottom and in the middle of the flap. The red and white spotted button goes into the middle of the flower.

11. Cut a small piece of interfacing (such as Decovil) and attach it in the middle back of the lining, about 2.5cm (1in) in from the bottom edge (check that it all matches up with the other half of the clasp set) and then attach the rest of the magnetic clasp set.

12. Fuse the lightweight interfacing (such as Decovil I Light) to the back of the embellished flap, straight over the top of the fusible wadding/batting. Lay the flap outer onto the flap lining with the right sides together and sew around the curved side only, leaving the flat top edge open. Clip the curve and turn out the right way; gently pull the flap into shape. Using white perle 8 cotton, make a running topstitch around the curved part of the flap.

The gusset

13. The gusset is a long strip with a dart in each end to give shape. Cut a strip from the red and white fabric (A) and also from the wadding/batting, measuring 5.5 x 41cm (2^1/$_4$ x 16in). Fuse the wadding/batting to the back of the fabric and then attach to a piece of foam interfacing the same size. Make a dart in either end (as shown on the pattern template).

14. Sew in the gusset, right sides together, to the bottom curve of the bag outer pieces and clip the curve so it doesn't pucker. You will need to trim the top of the gusset level.

The lining

15. Cut two pieces of red lining fabric and one red lining gusset. Put the dart in as you did for the outer gusset.

16. Make a lined patch pocket (see page 31). It doesn't have to be very big – around 10 x 8cm (4 x 3^1/$_4$in) is perfect; use fusible interfacing (such as S320).

17. Attach the pocket in the middle of the lining that will form the back of the bag. Use a coordinating thread and a narrow topstitch seam.

> ## Tip
> Cut a little tab of woven ribbon and slide it into the side of the patch pocket as a decorative tab.

18. Sew the lining front, back and gusset pieces together, right sides facing, leaving a gap in the bottom of the lining for turning the bag through.

The tabs

19. Cut a piece of red solid fabric to 20 x 12cm (8 x 4^3/$_4$in), interface with Bundfix tape on the wrong side and fold in half lengthwise. Fold the two raw edges to the centre and press in half. Topstitch each long side.

20. Attach a piece of woven ribbon to the centre. Cut the strip in half to make two tabs.

> ## Tip
> Remember to use different coloured threads in the top of the sewing machine and the bobbin. One needs to match the woven ribbon and the other needs to match the tab fabric.

21. Slip a 'D'-ring onto each and attach one to the top of the gusset on each side, right sides facing, aligning the raw edges. These will carry the strap.

The strap

22. Cut a piece of turquoise fabric B measuring 12 x 135cm (4³/₄ x 53¹/₄in); you may need to join a few pieces together. Fuse Bundfix tape to the back of it. Iron in half lengthwise. As you did for the little red tabs, fold the two raw edges to the centre crease and iron them. Close the strip with the raw edges trapped inside and topstitch along both long edges.

Putting it all together

23. Pin the flap to the back of the bag, right sides together and aligning the raw edges; sew it in place.

24. With the outer bag the right side out and the lining inside out, pull the lining on over the bag and line up the seams. Sew around the top edge, trapping the raw edge of the tabs and the flap as you sew.

25. Turn the bag out through the gap in the lining. Stuff the lining down into the bag. Topstitch around the top edge.

26. Place a rivet into the red tabs to keep the 'D'-rings in place.

27. Attach one end of the strap to the middle bar of the slider. Thread the other end through one of the 'D'-rings and then back through the slider to the other 'D'-ring. Sew it securely. The strap is now adjustable.

The embellishments

28. To make the bag charm, take the crochet flowers and layer them up. Sew the green button into the middle. You will need another felt flower too, and it is a good idea to have a couple to layer so that the ends of the ribbons are not visible.

29. Cut about 12cm (4³/₄in) of woven ribbon and thread it through the swivel clasp. Sew up the sides of the ribbon to make it a little more solid.

Tip

This step is necessary because this beautiful ribbon is actually quite fragile. Pull on the end of a scrap and see what I mean.

30. Hot glue the crochet flower motif to the felt flower. Hot glue the ribbon to the back. Thread a needle with perle cotton (white) and thread some beads on using a small one at the base to anchor. Attach this to the back of the charm. Cover the back with a second felt flower.

Dörte

Who doesn't love a bit of retro? For those old enough to remember, this saddle bag style was very big in the 1970s. It was usually made from tan or black hand-tooled leather, but fabric works well, too. This style is having its moment again right now.

Finished size: 30 x 28 x 7cm (12 x 11 x 2¾in), plus strap

The front

1. Using the template, cut a front section (A + B) from the jacquard (fabric A) and fuse it to a piece of wadding/batting (such as H630) the same size.

2. Using template B, cut the bottom feature from interfacing (such as Decovil). Fuse this to a piece of linen (fabric E) about 2.5cm (1in) larger all around. On the top curved edge, clip into the curves of the linen but don't clip all the way to the edge of the interfacing; on the side edges and bottom, trim back to the interfacing.

Tip

All of the action is on the inside curve on the linen trim, so that it where you need extra fabric and to clip. The outer edge can be trimmed to fit the interfacing as the raw edges will be taken care of in the seams.

3. Fold the clipped top edge over to the back of the interfacing and press. Some double-sided tape will help to keep it in position.

4. Lay the linen trim on top of the jacquard (both fabrics facing upwards) and position perfectly; pin. Attach with a narrow topstitch in a coordinating thread along the top curve of the linen.

5. The top band of the bag uses template piece C and is cut from the gingham fabric (D). Fuse this to a piece of wadding/batting (such as H630) and trim. Sew to the top of the bag; press.

6. Use the completed front as a template to cut two pieces of lining fabric.

7. The twist lock is sited 7cm (2³/₄in) down from the top edge in the centre. Reinforce the back of the area with a scrap of interfacing (such as Decovil) and then attach the male half of the lock (see page 15).

8. Sew the front of the bag to a piece of slightly larger foam interfacing with a narrow seam, then trim back.

The back

9. Construct the back in exactly the same way as the front, following steps 1–5.

10. Mark a zip box measuring 18 x 1cm (7 x ³/₈in), 4cm (1¹/₂in) down from the top edge on the gingham. The lining is red and white spot and measures 40cm deep by 22cm wide (15³/₄ x 8³/₄in). Install the zip with coordinating thread and construct the pocket (see pages 22–23). Attach the edelweiss charm to the zip pull.

11. Attach to a piece of foam interfacing with a narrow seam and trim.

Gather these supplies

Fabrics
- A: ½m (20in) warm grey jacquard with an alpine/deer pattern, for bag outer
- B: 40cm (15¾in) large red and white spotted fabric, for lining
- C: 40cm (15¾in) small red and white spot, for pockets, strap and flap linings
- D: 1 fat quarter red and white gingham, for the top band
- E: ½m (20in) brown melange linen, for flap centre and bag base

Interfacings
- ½m (20in) foam interfacing (such as Style-Vil)
- 1 fat quarter fusible interfacing (such as S320)
- ½m (20in) fusible wadding/batting (such as H630)
- ½m (20in) fusible interfacing (such as Decovil)
- 20cm (8in) heavy-duty interfacing (such as S133)
- Bundfix tape, 7cm (2¾in) wide
- 1 fat quarter lightweight fusible interfacing (such as Decovil I Light)

Everything else
- 1 medium silver twist lock set
- 18cm (7in) red zip
- 2.5cm (1in) silver bag slider
- 2 2.5cm (1in) silver rectangle rings
- Coordinating threads for topstitching
- Silver edelweiss charm
- Large edelweiss button
- Red felt heart
- Your usual sewing needs

The gusset

12. Cut a piece of jacquard (fabric A) using the gusset pattern piece. Fuse this to a piece of wadding/batting (such as H630). Cut a piece of heavy-duty interfacing (such as S133) 1cm ($^3/_8$in) smaller all around, and fuse it to the centre back of the fabric.

Tip

The gusset is tapered on the top – make sure that you echo this taper when cutting the interfacing.

---

13. Sew the gusset to a piece of foam interfacing with a narrow seam, then trim.

14. Sew the gusset to the bag outer front and back pieces, right sides facing, and trim the top.

The flap

15. Using template E, cut a shape from lightweight fusible interfacing (such as Decovil I Light). Fuse this to the back of a piece of linen (fabric E) and cut it out, leaving a seam allowance of 1cm ($^3/_8$in) all around. Cut into the curves of the linen, not cutting right back to the interfacing and, as you did in step 3, fold, press and tape the clipped edges to the back.

16. Using template D, cut a piece of gingham (fabric D), a piece of lining (fabric C), two pieces of lightweight interfacing (such as Decovil I Light) and a piece of wadding/batting (such as H630). Fuse the lightweight interfacing to the back of the outer and lining pieces and then fuse the wadding/batting to the back of one of the pieces. Trim if necessary and test the flap for fit (seam allowance differences can make a difference to how it fits, and it is easier to tweak now!).

17. Find the centre of the gingham flap piece and add the linen trim section on the top, with the right sides of both pieces facing up. Topstitch around the linen piece with coordinating thread and trim. Treat as one piece now.

18. Put the flap lining and flap outer pieces right sides together. Sew the sides and curved end leaving the straight top edge open.

19. Clip the curves and turn the right way out. Iron very carefully, making sure that the edge is perfect. Topstitch with coordinating thread and a very narrow seam.

20. Trim the open end and close with a narrow topstitch.

21. Attach the other half of the twist lock to the middle of the flap curve, carefully lining it all up with the half of the lock already in position (see page 15).

22. With the right sides facing and the raw edges aligned, sew the flap in place, centrally, to the top back of the bag.

The lining

23. You have two lining pieces already cut. Cut a gusset piece using the pattern piece, also from the spotted lining fabric.

24. Make two lined patch pockets – 20 x 15cm (4 x 6in) in size – from lining fabric and fusible interfacing (such as S320; see page 31).

25. Topstitch them narrowly to the right side of the lining pieces, centrally and about 4cm (1$^1/_2$in) from the top. Make a vertical seam or two to give them sections.

26. Sew the lining sides and gusset together as you did for the bag outer, but this time leave a gap in a bottom edge for turning through.

The strap

27. The strap is jacquard (fabric A) lined with small red and white spot. To achieve this, cut a piece of each 6 x 120cm (2$^1/_2$ x 47$^1/_4$in). Sew them together along a long edge.

28. Cut a piece of Bundfix tape 120cm (47$^1/_4$in) long and fuse it to the wrong side of the strap, lining the centre perforations on the tape with the seam in the middle. Fold the raw edges in (trim them back a bit if necessary) and topstitch four times with coordinating threads (see page 33).

29. Trim the ends. Attach one end of the strap to the centre bar of the bag slider.

The tabs

30. Cut a piece of Bundfix tape 12cm (4³⁄₄in) long, and a piece of red and white gingham to match. Fuse the tape to the back of the fabric. Fold the raw edges in, fold in half, then topstitch down both sides and twice more in the middle (see page 33).

31. Cut the tab in half to make two pieces and thread a rectangle ring onto each. Sew a tab centrally to the top of the gusset on each side, right sides facing.

Putting it all together

32. With the bag outer the right way out, check that everything is straight. Pull the inside-out lining on over the outer so that the right sides are together. Sew around the top edge and then turn out through the gap in the lining. Close the gap and stuff the lining down into the bag. Topstitch around the top edge with coordinating threads.

33. Attach the strap by threading the free end through a rectangle ring, back through the bag slider and then secure it at the other rectangle ring.

34. Lay the felt heart onto the front of the flap just above the twist lock (a bit of fabric glue will help it to behave). Sew the button onto the middle of the heart with shallow stitches. Try not to go all the way through the flap. This is easier with a longer needle.

Kirsten

This is a great everyday bag. It is hardworking and practical but still very stylish. I love the Scandi vibe suggested by the use of red and grey together – the result is a very grown-up bag!

Finished size: 34 x 29 x 10cm (13½ x 11½ x 4in), plus handles

The front

1. Using the template, cut the two mirror-imaged linen pieces from fabric A and fuse them to a piece of very lightweight interfacing (such as F220). Draw in the darts, cut out, and trim.

2. For the middle section of the front, cut one piece of fabric B measuring 17 x 29.5cm (6³/₄ x 11²/₃in). Fuse this to a piece of wadding/batting (such as H630) and trim. Also cut two pieces of lining fabric measuring 17 x 25cm (6³/₄ x 10in).

3. Make a 10 x 10cm (4 x 4in) patch pocket from fabric A and fusible interfacing (such as S320), lined with fabric D (see page 31). Using the same technique, also make a 12 x 5cm (4³/₄ x 2in) rectangular pocket flap.

4. Topstitch the pocket and flap to the middle of the interfaced central red panel, 5cm (2in) down from the top edge; position the flap about 15mm (²/₃in) above the top of the pocket. Attach a plastic snap fastener to close.

5. Position the zip face down on the straight edge of the right-hand linen panel, with the open end at the top, and a piece of lining over the top (right sides together).

6. Tack/baste the zip in place, then sew, tucking the end 'tail' out of the way.

7. Topstitch along the zip and lining so that the zip sits facing the side rather than upwards. Tack/baste the red centre panel and the other piece of lining to the other side of the zip. Sew this side, then topstitch to the lining.

8. Fold the red centre panel to the linen panel and pull the lining pieces in the other direction. Sew from the bottom of the bag right up to the end of the zip to close the gap there. Sew across the bottom of the pocket lining.

9. Take the opposite linen panel, the red centre panel and the two lining pieces and sew down the edge forming the left-hand side of the bag front and closing the pocket off on the left-hand side.

10. Press and trim the finished bag front panel, then pin to a piece of foam interfacing that is a little larger all around. Attach the bag front to the foam with a half-normal seam and then trim.

11. Using the front piece as a template, cut a whole piece of red fabric B for the back of the bag and interface with very lightweight interfacing (such as F220). Put to one side. Also cut two lining pieces the same size and put aside.

12. Sew in the darts on the front of the bag, right sides facing.

13. Tie a small piece of red ribbon into the zip pull.

Gather these supplies

Fabrics
- A: 40cm (15¾in) Essex yarn-dyed linen in charcoal, for bag front, front patch pocket and handles
- B: 50cm (½yd) red and white fabric, for front pocket and bag back
- C: 1 fat quarter grey fabric, for top band and inner patch pockets
- D: 1m (1yd) red and white fabric, for lining

Interfacings
- 1m (39½in) foam interfacing (such as Style-Vil)
- 1 fat eighth fusible interfacing (such as S320)
- 1m (39½in) very lightweight fusible interfacing (such as F220)
- Bundfix tape, 7cm (2¾in) wide

Everything else
- 2 18cm (7in) grey zips
- 4 40mm (1½in) rectangle rings
- 2m (79in) coordinating ribbon
- 3 black plastic snap fasteners
- 15mm (½in) magnetic clasp
- Coordinating threads for topstitching
- Glue stick
- 5mm (¼in) wide double-sided tape
- Water-soluble marker
- Your usual sewing needs

Tip

This whisper-weight F220 interfacing will hold the linen steady and stop it from fraying – its absolute favourite thing to do!

The back

14. Measure down 3cm (1¹/₄in) from the top edge, and centrally draw a zip box measuring 1 x 18cm (³/₈ x 7in).

15. Cut a piece of pocket lining fabric 22cm wide by 40cm (8³/₄ x 15³/₄in). Install the second grey zip and finish the pocket lining (see pages 22–23).

16. Add a small piece of ribbon to the zip pull.

17. Attach the bag back to a slightly larger piece of foam interfacing with a narrow seam, then trim back. Sew in the darts.

The bands

18. Cut two pieces of grey fabric (C) measuring 37 x 8cm (14¹/₂ x 3¹/₄in). Back each piece with very lightweight interfacing (such as F220).

19. Attach each band to a slightly larger piece of foam interfacing with a narrow seam and then trim back.

20. Attach a piece of ribbon along the centre of each piece by topstitching along both sides of the ribbon.

21. Attach a label to the right-hand side of the front band piece, centrally over the trim; sew it right sides facing, aligning the raw edges.

22. Sew a band piece to the top of the front and back panels.

23. With the right sides together, sew the front and back pieces of the bag together.

The handles

24. Cut a strip of linen (fabric A), 10 x 160cm (4 x 63in), and make a wide strap, interfacing it with Bundfix tape. Fold the raw edges in and hold them in place with some glue tape. This will make it so much easier to get a neat and professional finish. Channel quilt four times along the length (see page 33).

25. Cut four 10cm (4in) pieces off the end – to become the tabs – and then cut the remainder in half to form two handles.

26. Attach a folded tab enclosing a rectangle ring to each side of the bag, front and back, 7cm (2³/₄in) in from the outer edges. Sew with right sides facing, aligning the raw edges. Using your zip foot, sew a line under each rectangle ring on the tab, to stop it from moving around.

The lining

27. Cut two strips of lining fabric, 37 x 8cm (14¹/₂ x 3¹/₄in). Join a band to the top of each main lining piece cut in step 11.

28. Make two lined patch pockets (interface with a fusible interfacing such as S320), one for each side of the lining (see page 31). Attach to the middle of the lining with a narrow topstitch. Add vertical seams and plastic snap fasteners to combat sagging.

29. Add the magnetic clasp set centrally to the top edges of the lining band pieces, 3cm (1¹/₄in) down; first fuse a bit of interfacing (such as S320) to the back of the fabric where you plan to site the clasp, for extra strength (see also page 14).

> ### Tip
>
> The pockets cannot be too large, as you don't want them to get in the way of the slightly curved sides and base. Think about what you want to put into them and make them accordingly.

30. Sew in the darts.

31. Place the lining pieces right sides together and sew down the sides and around the base, leaving a 20cm (8in) gap in the bottom.

32. With the bag the right way out and the lining inside out, pull the lining over the bag and pin around the top edge, matching everything up. Sew around the top. Turn the bag out through the gap in the lining. Sew the gap closed.

33. Thread your handles through the rectangle rings and secure them by sewing close to the rings, as you did before.

Helge

I had an idea a year or two ago that it would be nice to have a Christmas-themed shopping bag just for use during December. The idea has taken off a bit, and a lot of people have liked the concept. Make one of these record-style bags for yourself and get into the Christmas spirit every time you use it!

Finished size: 32 x 37 x 7cm (12½ x 14½ x 2¾in), plus strap

The tabs

1. Cut 20cm (8in) of Bundfix tape, and a piece of fabric D, 20 x 10cm (8 x 4in). Fuse the tape centrally to the wrong side of the fabric. Fold the edges over the tape and then fold the whole thing in half; topstitch with coordinating thread twice down each side. Cut in half and enclose a rectangle ring in each. Put aside.

The strap

The strap is adjustable and you can make it as long as you need.

2. Cut a 130cm (51in) piece of Bundfix tape. Cut a strip of fabric A, 10 x 130cm (4 x 51in) – join strips together if your fabric isn't long enough. Fuse the Bundfix tape to the wrong side of the fabric and proceed to make the strap as for the tabs in step 1. Trim the ends of the strap and secure one end to the middle bar of the bag slider.

Tip

A glue stick can be very helpful for keeping the strap shut as you sew.

The flap

3. Begin by cutting a piece of sew-in wadding/batting to 40 x 45cm (15³/₄ x 17³/₄in). Using the template, draw the outline of the flap onto the wadding/batting with water-soluble marker.

4. You will 'colour in' this shape with fabrics using a quilt-as-you-go (QAYG) method. Begin with a scrap of one of the fabrics about 10cm (4in) square. Find a spot on the flap wadding/batting and, using a channel quilting style with lines about 1cm (³/₈in) apart, sew on the square.

5. Now take another scrap in a different colour and place it right sides together onto the first. Sew a normal seam. Open the scrap out and press it carefully and then channel quilt it as you did for the first piece.

6. Continue like this until the flap shape is covered with shapes, going over the outline to make sure that it is well filled. Then cut it out (because you have sewn scraps over the outline, lay the template over again and redraw the line so that you can see where to cut).

7. Cut a piece of lightweight interfacing (such as Decovil I Light) using the flap template and fuse it to the back of the flap panel.

Gather these supplies

Fabrics
- **A:** 40cm (15¾in) red and white Christmas print fabric, for strap, gusset and inner patch pockets
- **B:** 50cm (½yd) red, white and warm grey Christmas print fabric, for front and back
- **C:** 1 fat quarter solid red fabric, for under-flap pocket
- **D:** 30cm (12in) warm grey and white diamond print fabric, for flap and tabs
- **E:** 1m (1yd) warm grey Christmas print fabric, for linings
- Scraps of all of the fabrics for the quilt-as-you-go (QAYG) flap

Interfacings
- 1 fat quarter sew-in wadding/batting (such as #272 Thermolam)
- 50cm (20in) lightweight fusible interfacing (such as Decovil I Light)
- 1m (39½in) foam interfacing (such as Style-Vil)
- 1 fat quarter fusible interfacing (such as S320)
- 50cm (20in) fusible wadding/batting (such as H630)
- Bundfix tape, 7cm (2¾in) wide

Everything else
- Glue stick (optional)
- 2 25cm (10in) red zips
- 1 18cm (7in) red zip
- 2 grey plastic snap fasteners
- Medium silver twist lock
- 2 38mm (1½in) silver rectangle rings
- 1 38mm (1½in) silver bag slider
- Coordinating threads for topstitching
- Ribbon scraps for the zip pulls
- Your usual sewing needs

These fabrics came from the Makower Scandi Collection, in case you want to use the same or similar.

133

8. Cut a piece of lining fabric E, 40 x 45cm (15³/₄ x 17³/₄in) and fuse it to a piece of fusible wadding/batting (such as H630) the same size. Do not cut out yet.

9. With the right sides together, sew the flap front to the lining around the sides and bottom, leaving the top straight end open. Trim the lining now and then clip the curves on the bottom corners of the flap. Turn the right way out and then topstitch the sides and bottom with a coordinating thread.

10. Sew the short straight side with a half-normal seam and trim it. This raw edge will be hidden when the bag is constructed.

11. Attach the female half of the twist lock centrally at the bottom of the flap, 2cm (³/₄in) up from the bottom edge (see page 15).

The front

12. The bag front has a lined double patch pocket with plastic snap fasteners to keep it closed (refer to image opposite). Begin by cutting a piece of interfacing (such as S320) 20cm deep by 27cm wide (8 x 10³/₄in). Fuse this to the wrong side of a piece of fabric C that is 1cm (³/₈in) larger all around. Cut a piece of lining the same size as the fabric.

13. With the lining and pocket front right sides facing, sew around the very edge of the interfacing, leaving a turning gap on the bottom. Trim the seam allowance back to 'normal' and then clip the corners across. Turn the pocket the right way out through the gap and then press so that the edges are perfect.

14. Cut a bag front piece from fabric B: it measures 36cm deep by 33cm wide (14¹/₄ x 13in). Fuse a piece of wadding/batting (such as H630) to the wrong side and then use the rounded edges from the flap template to round the two bottom corners.

15. Find the vertical centre and then site the patch pocket centrally, 10cm (4in) up from the bottom of the bag. Secure it with a narrow topstitch in a matching thread; sew up the centre to create two equal-sized pockets.

16. Insert a zip pocket centrally, 3cm (1¹/₄in) down from the top edge (see pages 22–23). The pocket lining measures 30cm wide by 40cm deep (12 x 15³/₄in) and the zip is 25cm (10in) long. Mark a box 25 x 1cm (10 x ³/₈in); the top of the pocket lining will be flush with the top of the bag front.

17. Cut a small square of lightweight interfacing (such as Decovil I Light) – about 5cm (2in) – and fuse it to the wrong side of the bag just under the patch pocket. This will be used to reinforce the bag for the twist lock.

18. Lay the front bag piece onto a piece of slightly larger foam interfacing and attach with a half normal seam. Trim the foam.

19. Attach plastic snap fasteners to the top of the patch pocket.

20. Attach the other half of the twist lock to the front of the bag, 7cm (2³/₄in) up from the bottom edge (see page 15).

21. Tie a scrap of ribbon through the zip pull.

The back

22. Cut the back piece to the same size as the front, from fabric B. Round the corners as for the front, and fuse wadding/batting (such as H630) to the back.

23. Cut a piece of zip pocket lining 50cm deep by 32cm wide (20 x 12¹/₂in). Make a zip box 5cm (2 in) down from the top edge of the lining; use a 25cm (10in) zip and make a zip box measuring 25 x 1cm (10 x ³/₈in). The top of the lining will sit flush with the top edge of the back of the bag.

24. Attach the back to a piece of foam interfacing slightly larger all around with a narrow seam, and then trim back the foam.

> *Tip*
>
> You can make a patch pocket for the back if you need more storage. I put on a cute label instead.

25. Tie a scrap of ribbon through the zip pull.

The gusset

26. Cut a 9 x 100cm (3¹/₂ x 40in) gusset from fabric A, and interface it with fusible wadding/batting (such as H630). You will notice that the gusset is too long: I always make them a little bit longer than needed, just in case. You can trim the extra away when it is all in place!

27. Sew the gusset to a piece of foam interfacing slightly larger all around with a narrow seam and then trim back the foam.

The lining

28. Cut two pieces of lining fabric to 36 x 33cm (14$\frac{1}{4}$ x 13in) and round the bottom corners of both, as for your front and back pieces. Cut a gusset lining piece 9 x 100cm (3$\frac{3}{4}$ x 40in).

29. Make two patch pockets 20cm wide by 15cm deep (8 x 6in), using the same method as in steps 12–13.

30. Attach the pockets to the lining pieces, using a narrow topstitch: position one 6cm (2$\frac{1}{2}$in) down from the top on the front piece and the other 8cm (3$\frac{1}{4}$in) down on the back piece. To counteract sagging, sew vertical seams to divide them and make handy smaller pockets for things like your phone or some pens.

I next added a zip pocket on the back lining piece. This is an optional step – you may not need as many pockets as I do! – but if you do wish to add one here, the zip box measures 18 x 1cm (7 x $\frac{3}{8}$in), and was positioned 3cm (1$\frac{1}{4}$in) from the top edge. The lining fabric measured 26cm wide x 40cm long (10$\frac{1}{4}$ x 15$\frac{3}{4}$in), and the top of the lining sits flush with the lining of the bag to make things easier.

31. Mark the centre of each lining piece, then sew the front lining piece to the gusset, right sides facing; then sew the back piece to the gusset, leaving a large gap in the bottom for turning out. Trim back the gusset.

Putting it all together

32. Sew the front outer piece of the bag to the outer gusset, right sides facing. Then sew the back of the bag to the gusset, leaving no gaps. Trim back the gusset. Attach the flap centrally to the back panel, right sides facing, aligning the raw edges.

33. Attach a tab with a rectangle ring enclosed to each end of the gusset at the top, right sides facing, raw edges aligned.

34. With the outer bag the right way out and the lining inside out, pull the lining on over the outer and line up the top seams. Sew around the top edge leaving no gaps. Turn the bag out through the gap in the lining and then sew the gap closed.

35. Push the lining down into the bag and then topstitch around the top edge to secure it.

36. Put the adjustable strap on by bringing it through the rectangle ring on one side, back through the slider and then securing it at the other rectangle ring (see page 34).

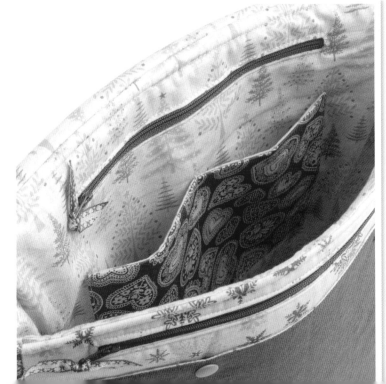

Karin

One question I've always asked myself is whether a baby bag should be made for mum or baby. Slightly odd question perhaps, but it seems such a shame to make a lovely bag that has only a short-term use. I have decided it should be all about Mum – after all, she has all the work to do and she deserves to have a nice bag to keep. Case dismissed!

Finished size: 47 x 34 x 11.5cm (18½ x 13½ x 4½in), plus handles

Front

The front of the bag has a large pocket, bound with green trim, which contains a smaller zipped pocket, that runs across the entire width of the bag and is secured to the main panel with a twist lock. We will start by making the main bag panel and then make the front pocket afterwards.

1. For the main fabric piece that forms the front of the bag (behind the large front pocket) cut a piece of fabric A, 51 x 36cm (20 x 14¼in). Cut a piece of sew-in wadding/batting (such as #279) slightly larger and pin them together, with the wadding/batting on the wrong side of the fabric. Quilt the fabric with a diagonal pattern and then trim the wadding/batting back to the size of the fabric.

Tip

Sometimes a large pocket, using all of the available space, is not the best way! Sometimes a slightly shallower one is more accessible when you are on the move and the bag is full and heavy.

---

2. Cut a piece of zip pocket lining (E) 40cm wide x 50cm deep (15³⁄₄ x 20in).

3. Find the vertical centre of the quilted front panel and use the 30cm (12in) zip to make a box zip pocket 3.5cm (1¹⁄₂in) down from the top edge in the centre (see pages 22–23). The top of the folded lining will sit in line with the top of the bag.

4. Attach a piece of ribbon to the zip pull to decorate.

5. On the centre back of the zipped, quilted panel, measure down from the bottom of the box zip by 5cm (2in) and fuse a piece of lightweight interfacing (such as Decovil I Light) in place. This is where the male half of the twist lock will go. Install the lock component centrally, 10cm (4in) down from the top of the fabric; just pull the lining out of the way to fit it (see page 15).

Gather these supplies

Fabrics
- A: 1m (1yd) floral, for the main front and back panels, handle trim and inner pockets
- B: 50cm (½yd) blue floral, for the zip panel, bag base and side panels of the large front pocket
- C: 1 fat quarter coordinating fabric, for the lower centre piece of the front pocket and the bag sides
- D: 1 fat quarter orange patterned, for the side pockets and the centre of the front pocket
- E: 1m (1yd) yellow floral, for lining
- F: 50cm (½yd) lime, for binding

Interfacings
- 2m (79in) foam interfacing (such as Style-Vil)
- 1m (39½in) heavy-duty interfacing (such as S133) for the base and sides
- 1 fat quarter fusible interfacing (such as S320)
- 50cm (20in) sew-in wadding/batting (such as #279)
- 1 fat eighth of lightweight interfacing (such as Decovil I Light)
- 25cm (10in) strip fusible wadding/batting (such as H630)

Everything else
- 4 large silver bag feet
- Medium silver twist lock
- 1.6m (64in) navy blue webbing
- Fabric glue
- Coordinating threads for topstitching
- 2cm (¾in) wide elastic
- 2 18cm (7in) navy zips
- Open-ended 61cm (24in) navy zip
- 30cm (12in) navy zip
- Scraps of ribbon
- Your usual sewing needs

Here is the list of Art Gallery Fabrics I used, in case you want to use the same:

- A: Collage Poise Deco
- B: Line Drawings Bluing
- C: Field Anecdotes Dark
- D: Ripples Coral
- E: Line Drawings Yellowed
- F: Lemonade

6. The front pocket has a few pieces, cut the following:

The front pocket cutting list

The side panels

2 pieces of fabric B: 28 x 17.5cm (11 x 7in)

The centre panel

1 piece of fabric D: 28 x 19cm (11 x 7½in)

The zip pocket

1 piece of fabric C: 19 x 21cm (7½ x 8¼in)

1 piece of lining (fabric E): 19 x 21cm (7½ x 8¼in)

1 piece of sew-in wadding/batting: 19 x 21cm (7½ x 8¼in)

From fabric F, create some bias binding for the zip, each side of the small zip pocket and the top of the whole pocket (see page 27).

Finally, cut a piece of sew-in wadding/batting to 51 x 28cm (20¼ x 11in) and a piece of lining fabric the same size.

7. To make the central panel, take the zip pocket fabric C (face up) and the corresponding sew-in wadding/batting and layer them together. Quilt together on the diagonal, with narrower channels than before. Bind the top edge with homemade binding. Tack/baste the edges together to keep them neat.

8. Sew the zip in along this top bound edge, stitching in the ditch of the binding with a coordinating thread. Turn the zip front over and attach the pocket lining to the back of the zip. This is a bit fiddly and it is easiest done by hand. It is worth it though, as it means that the zip tape is hidden.

9. Lay this zipped pocket piece onto the centre panel (fabric D) and pin with the zip flat and sitting above the pocket. Lay the binding along the top edge of the zip tape and topstitch down each side of the binding length to complete the pocket.

10. Trim the pocket and then join the two side pieces (fabric B) either side.

11. Press and lay onto the piece of sew-in wadding/batting. Channel quilt the side panels vertically with lines about 1cm (³⁄₈in) apart – this makes a nice textural contrast to the central diagonal quilting.

12. Cut a few more pieces of binding for the sides of the middle pocket and then topstitch these in place with coordinating thread, hiding the seams.

13. Prepare the large piece of lining fabric for the twist lock by reinforcing the back of it with a 5cm (2in) square piece of lightweight interfacing (such as Decovil I Light). Find the centre with a vertical crease and fuse the interfacing to the wrong side of the lining at the top. Don't leave a seam allowance. It isn't necessary and, this way, the seam from the binding will further strengthen it.

14. Install the twist lock 1.5cm (²⁄₃in) down from the top edge in the middle (see page 15). Lay the pocket section over the quilted bag front section to check that the two halves of the lock line up perfectly.

15. Lay the lining fabric and the quilted top panel wrong side facing. Pin and tack/baste together.

16. Trim the panel and bind the top edge with green binding.

17. Lay the completed pocket over the quilted front bag piece, close the lock, and tack/baste the layers together.

18. Place the two components onto a piece of foam interfacing slightly larger all around and attach with a very narrow seam. Trim the foam interfacing.

19. Attach a ribbon to the zip pull.

Back

20. Cut a piece of fabric A to 51 x 36cm (20 x 14$\frac{1}{4}$in) and a piece of sew-in wadding/batting slightly larger. Quilt the fabric panel as for the front panel of the bag and then trim back.

21. Cut a piece of lining 25cm wide by 50cm deep (10 x 20in) for the zip pocket.

22. Install a box zip centrally on the back panel, 4cm (1$\frac{1}{2}$in) down from the top, with one of the 18cm (7in) zips. The zip box will measure 18 x 1cm (7 x $\frac{3}{8}$in). Complete the pocket by folding the lining up and sewing the sides and top – the folded lining will sit at the top of the bag panel (see pages 22–23).

23. Attach the whole of the back panel to a piece of foam interfacing slightly larger all around with a narrow seam; trim the interfacing back. Attach a piece of ribbon to the zip pull.

Sides

24. Cut two pieces of fabric C that measure 14 x 36cm (5$\frac{1}{2}$ x 14$\frac{1}{4}$in). Pin these to a slightly larger piece of sew-in wadding/batting (such as #279) and channel quilt on the diagonal. Trim back the wadding/batting.

25. Cut two pieces of heavy-duty interfacing (such as S133) 1cm ($\frac{3}{8}$in) smaller all around than the quilted outers. Fuse to the wrong side of each panel in the middle so that you have a small margin all around.

26. Cut two pieces of foam interfacing slightly larger than each panel and attach with a narrow seam. Trim the excess foam.

27. To make the elasticated pockets, cut the pieces, as shown right.

28. Take one piece of fabric F, fold it in half lengthways and crease down the middle. Take a piece of fabric D and a piece of lining and place them right sides together. On one side (which will become the top), insert the folded fabric in between so that the raw edges are all at the top. Sew along the edge, trapping the four layers together. Open the pieces out and press. You should now have a lined pocket with a green casing at the top.

29. Sew down the sides of the pocket, completely missing the green casing at the top. Topstitch about 5mm ($\frac{1}{4}$in) underneath the casing. Trim and neaten the sides. Insert a piece of elastic into the casing and secure one end. Feed it through and secure at the other end too.

30. Pleat the base of the pocket so that it fits onto the side panel. Sew the pocket onto the side panel around the sides and bottom with a narrow seam. Repeat all of this for the other one.

31. Sew the front, back and side pieces together, right sides facing.

The elasticated side pockets cutting list

Two pieces of fabric D:
22 x 22cm (8$\frac{3}{4}$ x 8$\frac{3}{4}$in)

Two pieces of lining:
22 x 22cm (8$\frac{3}{4}$ x 8$\frac{3}{4}$in)

For the elastic casing

Two pieces of fabric F:
6.5 x 22cm (2$\frac{1}{2}$ x 8$\frac{3}{4}$in)

Two pieces of elastic: 12cm (4$\frac{3}{4}$in)

Base

32. Cut a piece of fabric B to 51 x 14cm (20 x 5$\frac{1}{2}$in), and a piece of sew-in wadding/batting slightly larger. Quilt together with diagonal channels and then trim to the same size.

33. Cut a piece of heavy-duty interfacing (such as S133) 1cm ($\frac{3}{8}$in) smaller all around than the quilted panel. Fuse it to the centre so that you have a generous seam allowance all around.

34. Sew this into the bag, right side facing out. As you sew, stop before you get to the edge each time so that you can achieve sharper corners. Ultra sharp corners are not going to happen because of the many layers, but by stopping sewing 5mm ($\frac{1}{4}$in) before the end, it is a bit better. Always reverse a few stitches each time to lock the seam because you don't want unravelling here.

35. Attach the four bag feet to the bottom – one in each corner, about 2.5cm (1in) in from the edges.

36. Cut a piece of foam interfacing to fit into the base. Trim it to fit and then hot glue it in place.

Straps and tabs

37. Cut the webbing in half to make two 80cm (31$\frac{1}{2}$in) pieces.

38. From fabric A, make a piece of straight binding (see page 28) roughly 2cm ($\frac{3}{4}$in) wide; it doesn't have to be exact in width, as long as you can see some of the webbing under it. It needs to be as long as the straps.

39. Use a piece of double-sided tape to adhere the binding down the length of each strap and then topstitch in place with a coordinating thread.

40. Attach a handle onto the front and back of the bag, 12cm (4$\frac{3}{4}$in) in from each end, right sides facing.

Top zip section

41. From fabric B and the lining fabric, cut two pieces 54 x 7cm (21$\frac{1}{2}$ x 2$\frac{3}{4}$in). Cut two pieces of foam interfacing slightly larger and adhere them to the back of the fabric B pieces. Trim the foam interfacing to size.

42. Prepare the zip by folding the end tapes (from the opening end) back and placing a tacking/basting stitch in to hold them. Leave the other end for the time being.

43. Tack/baste both short ends of the prepared fabric B strips under by about 1cm ($\frac{3}{8}$in). Make sure that your panels measure 51cm (20in) long when folded under so that they fit onto the top of the bag and don't go over.

> ### *Tip*
> This is a bit bulky because of the foam interfacing (it won't be in a minute when it is stitched down) so it won't behave if you just iron it. It is best if you use tacking/basting stitches rather than pins. You have an extra seam allowance to make it a bit easier. Clips might work for you too. It has to be perfect so spend some time on it.

44. With the lining piece and an interfaced outer piece right sides together, sandwich the zip in between. Line up the tucked-under ends at both ends of the zip. They have to be perfectly aligned because in a minute, they will be topstitched together. The opening of the zip goes right at one end and a bit of a tail on the other end is allowed to hang.

45. Sew along the length of the zip. Open out the outer and lining pieces and smooth everything. Pin, then topstitch along the short side, along the zip and down the other short side. Leave the other long raw edge open for now.

46. Repeat on the other side of the zip.

47. Measure the width of the top panel with the zip closed. It will be slightly too wide – this allows for seam allowance anomalies and it is better to have it too wide because you can always trim some away.

48. Take advantage of the zip's open end and undo it completely. With the right sides together, attach one half of the zip panel to each top side of the bag. Put the zip back together and check the fit, adjusting if necessary, before stitching in place.

> ### *Tip*
> In the final section, we will make a tab for the zip end and then it won't be open-ended any more. But for now, it is more convenient as it is.

Lining

49. To make the lining, cut the following:

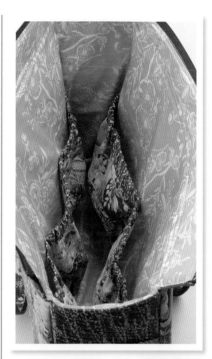

The lining cutting list

From fabric E, cut the following:

2 pieces: 48 x 35cm (19 x 14in) for the front and back

2 pieces: 13 x 35cm (5$^1/_8$ x 14in) for the sides

1 piece: 13 x 48cm (5$^1/_8$ x 19in) for the base

For the two inner elasticated pockets, cut:

From fabric A: 2 pieces 20 x 55cm (8 x 21¾in)

From fabric F: cut 2 pieces the same for lining

From fabric C: cut 2 casings 6.5 x 55cm (2½ x 21¾in); it is okay to join fabric pieces together to create the casing strips

2 pieces of elastic, 45cm (17¾in) long

For the two elasticated bottle holders, cut:

From fabric D: 2 pieces 6.5 x 20cm (2½ x 8in)

2 pieces of elastic, 15cm (6in) long

50. Fold the casing in half lengthways and press. Lay a pocket lining piece down (face up). Place the folded casing on top with the raw edges to the top and then lay the pocket outer on top (face down). Sew along the top, sandwiching the casing in the middle. Flip the sandwich open and press. Topstitch along the length just under the casing to keep the lining neat. Repeat for the other casing.

51. Trim the edges and pleat the base a bit so that the casing fits the width of the lining neatly. Pin each in place on a front and back lining panel.

52. Thread the elastic through the casing and tack/baste one end in place. Sew the pocket onto the lining, along the sides and bottom edge, anchoring the other end of the elastic in place as you sew up the side. Repeat for the other lining piece.

Tip

You will find that the elastic pulls the lining out of shape. You can combat this when it is in the bag by understitching into the interfacing, using the foam depth to your advantage.

53. Divide up the pockets with some vertical stitching – either in half or in thirds, or perhaps one of each to store different sized things.

54. To make each bottle holder, fold the fabric strips lengthways and right sides together; sew along the long open edge. Turn right side out and insert the elastic, anchoring at the ends and allowing the fabric to gather.

55. Sew each bottleholder in place, by the ends, about 10cm (4in) up from the bottom of each side lining piece.

Putting it all together

56. Attach the lining side pieces to the lining front piece, but when you do, stop 5mm ($\frac{1}{4}$in) from the bottom on each side. You need this gap so that the base fits properly.

57. Sew the back lining piece in place in the same way. You now have a 'tube' of fabric. Sew in the base, again, not sewing all the way to the edges to avoid puckering, and leaving a large gap along one side, so that you can turn the bag right side out.

58. With the lining inside out, pull it on over the top of the outer bag so that the right sides are together; sew around the top completely. Turn out through the gap in the lining base and then sew it closed it by hand.

59. Topstitch around the top edge to keep the lining down. Some understitching can help with this. Take advantage of the deep properties of the foam interfacing.

60. Make a tab for the end of the zip with a piece of fabric A, 5.5 x 12cm ($2\frac{1}{4}$ x $4\frac{3}{4}$in). Fold in half widthways (right sides together) and sew the sides to make a little bag. Turn out the right way and fold the raw edge in to make a square. Snip the end off the zip and slide the tab on. Sew around the perimeter.

> ## Tip
> It is a jolly good idea to sew a couple of times over the end of the zip just in case – you don't want it unravelling now that the bag is finished!

INDEX

Appliqué 16, 35, 39, 40, 53, 76, 85, 95, 117, 118

Beaded charms 43, 60, 69, 108, 122, 123
Beading 43
Brooches 42
Bundfix tape 12, 33, 53, 57, 63, 64, 67, 69, 71, 72, 73, 83, 85, 86, 95, 98, 101, 103, 107, 109, 117, 118, 121, 122, 123, 125, 126, 127, 129, 130, 133

Crocheted flowers 41, 79, 80, 113, 115, 121, 123

Embellishments 6, 9, 11, 16, 33, 35, 37, 39, 42, 57, 60, 85, 115, 118, 123
Embroidery stitches 35–38

Fabrics 8
Felts 9
Free-motion embroidery 16, 39, 40, 67, 76, 117, 118

Haberdashery 12
Handles 8, 13, 20, 32, 33, 51, 53, 57, 60, 63, 64, 65, 75, 76, 77, 85, 89, 90, 95, 98, 101, 103, 117, 118, 129, 130, 137, 140
Hardware 12, 13, 32

Interfacing 12, 13, 14, 15, 25, 26, 31, 32, 33, 49, 51, 53, 54, 57, 58, 59, 63, 67, 68, 71, 75, 76, 79, 80, 83, 85, 86, 89, 93, 95, 96, 98, 101, 102, 104, 107, 108, 109, 110, 113, 114, 117, 121, 122, 125, 126, 129, 130, 133, 134, 137, 139, 140, 142

Labels 6, 16, 44–45, 72, 75, 76, 96, 107, 108, 113, 114, 121, 130, 134

Pockets 12, 13, 20, 22–23, 28, 31, 44, 57, 58, 65, 75, 83, 85, 95, 96, 97, 101, 102, 107, 113, 129, 137
  Elasticated pockets 139, 142
  Patch pockets 16, 19, 49, 51, 54, 57, 60, 67, 68, 71, 72, 73, 75, 77, 79, 80, 83, 86, 89, 93, 95, 98, 101,
107, 110, 113, 114, 118, 122, 125, 126, 129, 130, 133, 134, 135, 137, 138, 142
  Zip pockets 50, 59, 64, 67, 68, 71, 86, 90, 97, 101, 103, 108, 110, 114, 122, 125, 130, 133, 134, 135, 137, 138, 139
Pompoms 60

Straps 13, 16, 32, 33, 34, 49, 51, 53, 54, 57, 60, 63, 64, 67, 69, 71, 72, 73, 79, 80, 83, 85, 86, 89, 90, 95, 96, 98, 101, 103, 107, 109, 111, 113, 115, 118, 121, 122, 123, 125, 126, 127, 130, 133, 135, 137, 140

Tabs 26, 32, 33, 34, 51, 64, 65, 68, 69, 71, 72, 73, 76, 83, 89, 90, 95, 98, 101, 103, 109, 110, 111, 113, 115, 117, 122, 123, 127, 130, 133, 135, 140, 143
Techniques
  Applying bias binding 28
  Applying piping 30
  Clipping, notching, cutting corners 26
  Inserting patch pockets 31
  Installing magnetic snaps 14
  Installing twist fasteners 15
  Installing zips 22–23, 24
  Lining 19, 20
  Making bias binding 27
  Making box corners 25
  Making piping 29
  Making straps and tabs 32, 33, 34
  Patchworking 21
  Seaming 18
Threads 10
Trims 11, 53, 63, 75, 77, 80, 83, 86, 90, 95, 102, 125, 126, 137

Webbing 16, 32, 89, 90, 95, 96, 97, 137, 140

Zip-free bags 53, 75, 79, 117
Zips 12, 16, 22–23, 24, 43, 49, 50, 57, 59, 63, 64, 65, 67, 68, 69, 71, 75, 79, 85, 86, 89, 90, 95, 96, 97, 98, 101, 102, 103, 104, 107, 108, 109, 110, 111, 113, 114, 117, 121, 122, 125, 129, 130, 133, 134, 135, 137, 138, 139, 140, 143

144